THE INSIDER

One of the highest run getters in Ranji trophy cricket, Aakash Chopra is a well-known former Indian cricketer, television commentator, columnist and author. Aakash writes regularly for ESPNcricinfo, *Mid-Day* and Starsports.com. In 2009, Chopra wrote his first book, the critically acclaimed *Beyond the Blues: A First-Class Season Like No Other*. His second book *Out of the Blue: Rajasthan's Road to the Ranji Trophy* was released in 2011.

THE INSIDER

Decoding the Craft of Cricket

AAKASH CHOPRA

Harper Sport

ESPNcricinfo

First published in India in 2015 by Harper Sport
An imprint of HarperCollins *Publishers*

HarperCollins Publishers India, Cyber City, Building 10-A, Gurugram,
Haryana-122002, India
www.harpercollins.co.in

2 4 6 8 10 9 7 5 3 1

P-ISBN: 978-93-5136-566-2
E-ISBN: 978-93-5136-567-9

Typeset in 10.5/14 Electra LT Std by
R. Ajith Kumar

Printed and bound at
MicroPrints India, New Delhi

MIX
Paper
FSC
FSC™ C218906

This product is made of FSC®-certified and other controlled material.

HarperCollins Publishers, Macken House, 39/40 Mayor Street
Upper, Dublin 1, D01 C9W8, Ireland

For my daughter, Aarna

CONTENTS

FOREWORD

Twenty years from now—I will venture confidently, and I hope not to offend him with this—Aakash Chopra, the cricketer, will have receded significantly from public memory, and no one will bear greater responsibility for that than he himself. Cricket fans, by then, will know him for his insights that enhance their understanding of the game, and in that he will be in the elite company of a small band of cricketers whose media work has brought them greater renown than has their playing of the game.

It is Aakash the writer I have always known. It was a newspaper column by him that first drew my attention, and he has written for us ever since, starting with a column on domestic cricket in *Wisden Asia Cricket* magazine in the first half of the 2000s. I think it was not until 2007 that I met him in person, and I remember one of my early conversations with him vividly. It was at Lord's and it involved Sachin Tendulkar.

Earlier that day, Tendulkar had been dismissed lbw by Monty Panesar, the England left-arm spinner, who had famously claimed him the same way as his first-ever Test wicket a year and a half before, in Nagpur, and then asked Tendulkar to autograph the match ball. The inscription read: 'Once in a blue moon, never again!' Naturally, at Lord's, Panesar's joy was uncontainable, and the matter also became the talking point of the day. Prima facie, the evidence was that Tendulkar had offered his pad to a straight ball with no apparent intent to play a stroke, and analysts and commentators had spent considerable time discussing what he did wrong.

Aakash made me see the dismissal in a different light.

Tendulkar, he said, had done the right thing. Panesar had been turning the ball away quite sharply, and was being further aided by the unique slope at Lord's. In such cases the natural instinct of a top-order batsman is to play outside the line of the ball to avoid the edge. And the ball that pinned Tendulkar was bowled with the routine left-arm orthodox action, and not as an arm ball designed to straighten. But as it sometimes happens in cricket, the ball created its own equation with the surface and charted its own course, and the batsman's instinct to push the pad outside to make it appear that the impact had been outside the line of off stump had made it seem that Tendulkar hadn't offered a stroke. I watched a replay that night and it began to make sense. But I did wonder why no else picked up on it.

Most cricketers possess a degree of comprehension of the technical aspects of the game, but cricket is a sport of many skills, and each of them – batting, bowling and fielding – contains multitudes. Even within something seemingly as straightforward as fielding, there are numerous specializations: fielding at slip requires a different technique, and temperament, than patrolling covers; a catch at forward short-leg, as Aakash will know first-hand, is hugely different from taking one at the boundary. It takes a little more than just playing the game to develop a composite and intimate understanding of all the aspects of cricket, and to then be able to articulate that knowledge in a manner that is easily comprehensible to fans. Aakash has that rare and exceptional gift. Rather, he has developed it assiduously. He has the keenest of eyes, an enquiring mind, and an ability to construct a big picture by zooming in on little things.

To add to this, he has given himself another big advantage: he takes his career in the media seriously. Many cricketers, particularly in India, view their role in the media as an extension of their playing career, and believe that their deeds in the field and standing in the game should carry them through. That Aakash's international career didn't reach the heights that some of his India teammates did perhaps got him thinking of media as a serious career option, but even during his playing days, he took his writing seriously. Unlike many of his contemporaries, his transition has been in reverse to the normal course, going from writing to television, and I dare suggest that it has helped develop his thinking. From the outset, he has written his pieces himself and never let his ego come in the way of a rewrite when one has been warranted. A few years ago, I told him that he could become our cricket correspondent after he gave up playing. He is the only Indian cricketer you could think of that way.

The Insider has been one of ESPNcricinfo's longest-running series, and it is remarkable how many of the pieces are timeless. The best of them are contained in the pages of this book, which provides an elegant treatise on the science and art of cricket, but is hardly academic. That this is the first of ESPNcricinfo's five titles in as many years by a single author should tell you something about Aakash Chopra.

Sambit Bal
Editor-in-chief
ESPNcricinfo

SECTION ONE

MIND GAMES

PREPARATION – PART I

Tillakaratne Dilshan amazed everybody when he scooped the ball over the wicketkeepers' heads off the quicker bowlers earlier in 2010. That innovative shot was the toast of 2010's World T20. It is a tough shot that requires eyes and nerves, which Dilshan has in heaps.

It might have seemed that Dilshan was responding to the then-and-there demand of T20 cricket, but the scoop is far from a spur-of-the-moment shot. It is a result of a lot of work in the nets. Dilshan had been practising the scoop since the first edition of the IPL, but he didn't use it in matches till he had mastered it and was sure he could execute it to perfection. Such mastery might look effortless and spontaneous, but it can only come out of a lot of practice.

Cricketers, and I suppose professionals in any field, put a lot of thought and effort into preparation. Like they say, 'Failing to prepare is like preparing to fail.' I am a firm believer in preparing thoroughly before embarking anything new, be it a season, a match or an innings.

When I talk about the importance of preparation, images of M.S. Dhoni and R.P. Singh playing badminton, or Ricky

Ponting and Brendon McCullum playing golf might come to my mind. If preparation really is that important, what were these guys doing? Admittedly it was during the off season. Why weren't they resting at home, recouping for the next season instead?

It is a myth that cricketers should rest during the off season. The off-season routine at the highest level of the sport involves physical activity, but preferably something other than cricket. Believe it or not, playing cricket constantly beyond a certain limit pushes you away from the game. You don't feel like holding the bat again or rolling your arm over to bowl yet another tiresome delivery. The limbs, and more importantly the mind, get so tired that the body craves time away from cricket. This is why after the initial phase of complete rest, which doesn't last more than a few days, we are advised to get involved in some kind of physical activity. It could be swimming, tennis, badminton or any other sport we choose. Anything but cricket. The idea is to keep the body in motion while resting the muscles involved in cricket.

After a few weeks of this, we start adding gym workouts in our schedule. My dad once told me something he learnt in his days with the Indian Air Force: 'The more you sweat in peace, the less you bleed in war.' It holds true in cricket. Cricketers have to be regulars in the gym even during the off season.

Workouts for cricketers are focused on maintenance rather than on putting on muscle and getting stronger. During the off season we work on the parts of the body that were found wanting in the previous season or need to be worked on to improve in the next one. Even if no amount of hard work in the gym can guarantee an injury-free season, the chances of successfully enduring the rigours are higher with a stronger and fitter body.

Most people think cricketers have a merry time when there is no cricket, when in fact they are actually sweating it out in the gym. Some players also practise yoga during the off season to strengthen the mind.

Then comes the next phase, 'pre-season', where the focus switches back to the skill aspect of the game. In this day and age, where there are hardly any long breaks between seasons, pre-season starts almost immediately after the active recovery is finished. This is the time to go back to the drawing board and work on the areas we were found lacking in during the previous season. We look at old videos—of days when we were batting at our best—and compare them with the latest ones. The future plan of action is decided based on what the videos reveal. Such analysis also helps fix bad habits that players tend to pick up during the season: playing across the line, the head falling over and so on. We need to be careful not to let these habits become part of our skill set. Watching videos and taking inputs from coaches and senior teammates helps eradicate any such habits.

During the season, the focus is on strengths, while being aware of shortcomings, but the off season is exactly the opposite. Since there is hardly any time to rectify mistakes during the season, we look for ways to succeed despite the faults; but those areas need to be addressed and pre-season is the time to do that. I have no doubt that the English batsmen who were found wanting against short-pitched bowling both against Mitchell Johnson and Ishant Sharma will be putting in hours in the nets to get that in order.

The next bit of preparation is based on what is coming next once the season starts. Are we going to play Test cricket or the shorter formats? In which part of the world? Against what opposition? Such questions determine our action plan.

In 2009, I attended a camp in Bangalore, just before India's Test tour to Sri Lanka. Muttiah Muralitharan was expected to be the biggest threat—we didn't know much about Ajantha Mendis back then—and we had sessions where we asked the off-spinners to bowl into the footmarks from a shorter distance. This way even the local boys managed to add spin and pace to the ball. We practised stepping out to get to the pitch of the ball and then playing along the ground. We also practised the forward-defensive shot, along with padding the ball away if it was too wide outside the off stump. When we were leaving for Australia, the practices featured negotiating short-pitched deliveries, either against a bowling machine or against bowlers bowling from 18 yards away.

Sanath Jayasuriya and Romesh Kaluwitharana practised clearing the in-field against bowling machines for weeks before the 1996 World Cup. Matthew Hayden was told well in advance about his inclusion for the tour to India in 2001. For months leading up to the tour, he practised the sweep and using his feet against the spinners. To handle Shane Warne's leg spin from round the stumps, Sachin Tendulkar got leg-spinners in Mumbai to bowl at him from round the stumps into the rough.

Such groundwork can only be done during the off season. Once the season starts you have to prepare on a day-to-day basis. In the next chapter, I will focus on all that goes into preparing before a match, an innings or a tournament.

PREPARATION – PART II

The first time I met the entire Indian team as an India cricketer was for a team meeting in a hotel room in Ahmedabad in 2003. We were about to start a series against New Zealand and the team was assembling after a break.

Coach John Wright started proceedings with the objectives for the new venture, which he also put up on the whiteboard. Next, Sourav Ganguly, then captain, spoke about how the team was shaping up and the areas we needed to work on. I had attended several team meetings in the past and this one was no different up until then. The similarity, though, ended there.

The team was then split into two groups, batsmen and bowlers. We were told to go into different corners and discuss the game plans for the two Test matches against New Zealand. While the batsmen spoke about the New Zealand bowling and marked out Daniel Vettori as the main threat, our bowlers analysed their batting.

Since I had played against the Kiwis in the warm-up games, I became the chief contributor among the batsmen. Sachin Tendulkar and Rahul Dravid would add some details to my narrative about a particular bowler. Obviously they were well aware of what was coming and allowed me to talk to brush up their memory and probably to make me feel comfortable.

It was just one of the many meetings I would attend over the next year with the team. On the eve of the match we got together once again, and this time Wright and Ganguly had specific plans for the opposition. We were again split into our two groups and asked to write down our plans and key points.

The idea of involving everyone in the decision-making process is to make them feel responsible. It is always easier to follow a plan that you have been a part of, as compared to one that is thrust upon you.

Batsmen were shown videos of every New Zealand bowler, and the senior players kept giving valuable inputs on their strengths and weaknesses and how to handle them. Bowlers had the more tedious job of going through every opposition batsman's strength (to avoid bowling in those areas) and the areas in which he was vulnerable (to try and get him out or contain him).

Batting is mostly about an individual against another, but bowlers need to complement each other at all times. If one bowler goes awry, the entire plan can collapse. For example, Steve Waugh was vulnerable on the front foot at the start of his innings, and the plan would be to keep bowling full to him, but if one bowler bowled him a few short-pitched deliveries, Waugh would be up and running and then it would be difficult to stop him.

We would also come up with a theme for the tour. The entire team would decide on a theme to reflect the goal for that particular tournament or series. 'Now or never' was the theme in the 2003 World Cup, while for the series in Australia in 2003-04 the motto was 'Change the trend'.

That was just a glimpse of how team meetings are at the highest level. But things are quite different one level lower. Most team meetings in first-class cricket revolve around the senior players reminding everyone of the importance of the game, and some motivational stuff. Analysing the opposition in detail rarely happens: there is very little data available for analysis and for some strange reason we are not intent on using whatever little we have. While most first-class teams have employed video analysts to cover their matches and practice sessions, the footage ends up becoming a tool only to analyse that team's own batting and bowling.

Most coaches at this level—barring a few—are quite old school. One such coach, an ex-India all-rounder, once claimed that a player should remember the strengths and weaknesses of every opponent he had ever played against. This sounds ridiculous, but that is exactly what certain team meetings are all about: you may not agree with everything being said, but it is all part of a larger plan.

Coming back to international cricket, it is important to emphasize here that the preparation is different for different forms of the game.

Tests

Test cricket is a lot about endurance and competing over five days and hence the preparation is customized to suit that requirement. Batsmen bat for longer in the nets and hit balls thrown down to them until they are absolutely satisfied.

You will see a lot of batsmen—like Laxman used to do those days—doing specific drills with heavy plastic balls on a concrete surface to handle short-pitched stuff. Similarly a lot of batsmen practise playing the defensive shot and also driving along the ground. Sehwag and Tendulkar, for example, would keep their leg guards on for hours after their batting got over, just to get used to wearing them for longer durations.

Bowlers, on the other hand, do most of their work at least a couple of days before the match. They bowl long spells in the nets, hitting specific areas. They then go into energy-conservation mode on the eve of the match, bowling only a few balls at full throttle and focusing primarily on their rhythm and shape instead. A bowler's workload during a Test is a lot more than a batsman's and hence the conservative approach.

Fielding drills are also designed to meet the demands of the game. There is a lot of emphasis on close-in catching while preparing for the longest version. Test cricket is all about specialists and that is true of fielding as well. People who are specialists in fielding at slip practise dives and catches for a good thirty to forty minutes, while bowlers practise fielding and catching in the deep. And people like me start with the slips, with everyone else, and finish with short sessions at short leg and silly point.

ODIs

This format is far more dynamic than Test cricket and hence the demands are different as well.

Batsmen bat in the nets to imaginary field positions, looking to score runs as they do. They get feedback from the bowlers to determine the number of runs a stroke would have fetched. Though they tend to disagree on most occasions, it helps add a healthy sense of competition. After playing a few rounds of conventional cricket, batsmen try to innovate and go over the top consistently. At times they bat in pairs and rotate the strike every few deliveries.

Bowlers, on the other hand, bowl even shorter spells, but practise bowling yorkers and slower ones, both in the nets and outside, challenging the batsmen to score over six to seven runs an over.

Fielding is also more dynamic in this format. There is a lot of emphasis on stopping the singles inside the thirty-yard circle, and almost everyone practises fielding in the deep as well.

T20s

The preparation here involves everything that one does while preparing for the fifty-over matches, with a few more innovations. The batting in the nets gets even shorter.

At Kolkata Knight Riders, we had four nets operating simultaneously—one for the fast bowlers, one for the spinners, and two bowling machines set at different speeds and lengths for the batsmen. We would get only four minutes of batting in each net. The idea was to get into the habit of maximizing the number of balls we played.

Then there is a lot of focus on key hitting areas. John Buchanan once asked me to hit everything across the line for the entire duration of my batting. The purpose of the exercise was to develop a new shot and get the mind and body accustomed to playing a stroke that had been alien to it in the past.

Bowling in T20 is along similar lines. No one is asked to bowl more than twenty-four balls in a session, especially not on the eve of a match. But special sessions for bowling yorkers, slower ones and bouncers are arranged almost every day. Spinners are encouraged to lower the trajectory without increasing the pace too much.

Fielding drills are more or less exactly like the ones used in fifty-overs cricket.

PREPARATION – PART III

What does Matthew Hayden do sitting on the pitch on the eve of a match? Does he meditate sitting there? And why does Rahul Dravid shadow-practise his shots at both ends? Hasn't he played enough in the nets? Chris Gayle also does the same thing, albeit in the middle of the pitch. What are these guys up to and what is the rationale behind these rituals?

Firstly, it is quite clear that all of them use an extremely important tool for preparation: visualization. Hayden visualized everything, good and bad, that could happen in a match, so as not to be surprised during the match. All of us, knowingly or unknowingly, do it.

I had my formal introduction to this technique just before the first Test against Australia in Brisbane in 2003. John Bell, an Australian coach I had met in Holland, told me about its application and importance. He told me to walk out from the dressing room on the eve of the match assuming that I was walking out to bat on the first morning of the game.

I had to psyche myself into seeing the packed stadium, the Australian team waiting in the middle along with the two umpires. I also had to imagine my partner, Virender Sehwag, was walking alongside me. Then I did my ritual, running a couple of mock runs, before settling in to take strike. To avoid looking completely insane, I skipped the part where I asked the imaginary umpire for a leg-stump guard. Apart from that, I did everything I would in the real match. I mentally drew a line just outside the off stump, to use as a marker for letting balls go. Anything pitched outside that line would be allowed to go through to the keeper and the rest were to be played. Then I would stand in my stance and visualize all the Australian bowlers running in and bowling in different areas. It is a routine I have followed ever since.

Ground reality

Every ground and track has a different feel and the earlier you get used to it the better. Batsmen identify certain shots for certain tracks. For example, on slow and low tracks you realize the need to get on to the front foot as much as possible and play with a straight bat. Similarly, on tracks with more bounce and pace, you prepare yourself to stay on the back foot and play horizontal bat shots. That is exactly why players shadow-practise while standing in the middle. Bowlers also identify the areas they will be expected to bowl in, and do mock run-ups to get a feel of the approach to the stumps.

Individual approach

Batting and bowling in the nets on the eve of the match is strictly according to each individual's liking. No one tells you to bat in the nets if you aren't comfortable, and the support staff does everything to help you get into the groove. Rohan Gavaskar, for example, wouldn't play a single ball in the nets, while Virender Sehwag always liked a long hit. Similarly, Gautam Gambhir needed his throw-downs before every match, while Sachin Tendulkar's batting in the nets depended purely on how he was feeling about his game at that point of time. While Sachin didn't bat too often in the nets during the 2003-04 series, when he did, he made someone bowl at him from fifteen yards most of the time.

There was one extraordinary instance of Dravid and Viru missing the practice session and watching a movie instead. It was before the memorable Adelaide Test in 2003. Sometimes, simply unwinding is the need of the hour.

At the end of the practice session, most batsmen take their match bats with them to the hotel. Some batsmen shadow-practise religiously in their rooms. Others just want the bat handy in case they feel like doing so.

Sleepless nights

Sachin didn't sleep well for fifteen days leading up to the match against Pakistan in the 2003 World Cup. He would stay awake planning how to handle each bowler. He confused that he played the entire innings in his head way before it happened on the field. Gautam, meanwhile, admitted that he couldn't sleep the night before the 2007 T20 World Cup final.

You often find cricketers sitting together till very late on the eve of a match. That is to ensure that the moment they walk into their rooms they fall asleep. The anxiety doesn't let your mind rest and that makes it very difficult to sleep. There is also the tendency to get up a few times during the night to check if you have slept through the alarm, only to find that dawn is still a few hours away.

A common dream for batsmen plays out something like this: a wicket has fallen and you are slated to go in next. But you haven't put on your leg guards and therefore panic sets in. You try your best to get ready but something or the other always goes wrong. In reality, gearing up is a two-minute exercise that has been done a million times, but then dreams seldom follow a logical pattern.

The morning of the match

Every player has his own routine on the morning of a game. Some, like Dravid, wake up well in advance, read newspapers and have breakfast before boarding the bus. Others sleep till the last possible minute and rush to the bus, grabbing a muffin on the way. Then there are those who indulge in incessant chatter all the way to the ground; they often occupy the last rows of the bus. Others, like Sachin, listen to music. These routines depend a lot on temperament: some can't handle the anxiety and hence rush through everything, while others want everything to happen peacefully.

After reaching the ground

Almost everyone rushes to the pitch at the centre immediately after getting to the field. Although nothing dramatic can happen, since you have seen the track the previous day, you need to be certain. It is like going through your notes one last time before an exam. You want to be 100 per cent certain that you didn't misread the pitch.

If it is an ODI or the start of a Test, there is the eternal wait for the toss. While one part of you wants it to be delayed for another couple of hours so you can hit a few more balls against throw-downs, the other part wants to be done with the suspense. Openers and fast bowlers watch the toss with great interest, and depending on the result of the toss, either prepare or relax.

Instead of warming up with cricket, most teams prefer playing a different, non-contact sport, like volleyball, just before the game. It lightens the atmosphere and helps you ease into the match day. Contact sports like football and touch rugby are generally avoided because the chances of getting injured are higher. Dhoni vehemently disagrees with my hypothesis and hence the Indian team is seen playing football almost every single match day.

Batting first

The environment in the dressing room becomes a lot quieter if your team is batting. Even though the bowlers slip into a relaxing mode, they avoid making unnecessary noise. Both the openers and the No.3 batsman are left alone. Everyone wishes the openers luck as they go through their last little routines before stepping on to the field. But there are some batsmen who don't like to be wished before walking out to bat. (One such was Sunil Gavaskar.)

Some batsmen will watch every single ball being bowled, as they wait their turn, either on TV or from the balcony, and then there are others who would read newspapers and magazines (Mohammad Azharuddin) or sleep (Sir Vivian Richards) while waiting for their turn to bat. V.V.S. Laxman likes to listen to music, while Yuvraj Singh prefers chatting.

I can't stop myself from watching. Thank god I was an opener.

Bowling first

While batsmen relax, the bowlers are required to be on the field ten minutes before the start of the game to warm up. But bowlers have the luxury of easing into the match, as they are not absolutely required to be at their very best right from the beginning. One mistake doesn't mean the end of the innings for them; an advantage that gets evened out with the heavy workload they have to bear. Their planning and plotting happens more on the field and during the match.

The opening batsmen start their preparation again when the opposition loses its eighth or ninth wicket. You see them standing in their stance and looking down the pitch every now and then. They also tend to go quieter in the field after the loss of the ninth wicket.

My endeavour through these three chapters on preparation was to tell you what goes into the making of a good ball, a marvellous catch, an unsparing shot, a great cricketer. I hope that from now on every time you see a batsman fail or a bowler bowl a half volley, you remember that lack of performance is not necessarily because of lack of preparation. It is just that, in the game of cricket, like in any other walk of life, it is only human to err.

READING THE BATSMAN

What if a bowler could read a batsman's mind? What if he could predict how a batsman would play before even bowling a ball to him or having watched him play? Wouldn't it bolster his chances, give him leeway to plan and buttress his skills?

Some may call it wishful thinking, others a secret science, but often, just looking at the grip with which a batsman holds his bat tells you something about his shot preferences and the way he stands may help you place your fielders.

Will a batsman be a good driver of the ball or be more comfortable scoring off the back foot? Will he prefer scoring runs through the on side or the off? It is important to observe the finer nuances of a batsman's grip, stance and back-lift to size him up and plan accordingly. While it may seem utterly useless in this day and age of exhaustive analysis based on video footage which is available to almost all professional teams, observation was one of the tools players relied heavily on in the past, and it continues to be useful.

The grip

Most batsmen playing professional cricket hold the bat correctly with regard to the Vs made by thumbs and forefingers. The top hand is firmer and the V its thumb and forefinger make opens out towards the outer edge of the bat, while the bottom hand plays only a supporting role.

A correct grip allows a proper downswing, which in turn enables a batsman to play the ball with the full face of the bat. The right grip is also imperative if you want to play the entire range of shots.

While the basics remain the same, a lot of batsmen do enough with the grip to give some information away. For instance, Sanath Jayasuriya held the bat close to the bottom of the handle, and Adam Gilchrist higher up. Now the coaching manual recommends that one hold the bat in the middle of the handle, but to say that successful players like these two didn't hold the bat correctly would be grossly incorrect. While there are pros and cons to each approach, it all boils down to what suits your game best.

Holding the bat closer to the bottom gives you more control and helps you generate more power at the point of impact. In such cases, since the bottom hand becomes dominant very often, you don't need a high backlift to hit the ball long and hard. That is why Jayasuriya was ever so good with his short-arm jabs. Such players generally are more comfortable on the back foot and horizontal bat shots are their bread and butter. The flip side of holding the bat close to the base of the handle is that the arc of the downswing gets radically smaller, which in turn reduces the reach and makes driving off the front foot that much difficult. But some players are exceptions to this rule. Sachin

Tendulkar held the bat close to the bottom of the handle but has managed to overcome this shortcoming with ease.

On the contrary, Gilchrist's batting was built on the extension of the arms and holding the bat high on the handle complements the extension. With this grip, the arc of the downswing becomes bigger and hence increases the reach of the batsman. Lower-order batsmen tend to prefer this grip to enhance their reach. That is how the phrase 'using the long handle' was coined. The flip side of such a grip is that you may not have enough control and you have to rely on the downswing to generate power. Players with such grips prefer playing on the front foot and can also be a little circumspect against quick short-pitched bowling. Gilchrist, like Tendulkar, was an exception here.

Then there were those like Javed Miandad, who had a gap between the top and bottom hands. The textbook recommends keeping the hands close to each other on the handle, to ensure that they move in unison. Yet Miandad's grip allowed him to manoeuvre the bowling and milk it for singles, though he possibly sacrificed some fluency in the bargain.

The stance

If the grip on the bat is the first giveaway, the manner in which a batsman stands is the second. While the coaching manual recommends the feet be about a shoulder span apart, plenty of batsmen have toyed with different options to suit their game.

People who stand with their feet too close to each other are often good back-foot players and the ones with wider stances are generally stronger on the front foot. Here too, there are snags:

you lose some balance if both feet are too close and too wide apart results in lack of foot movement.

A stance that is too side on or too open chested also tells you a bit about the strengths and weaknesses of a batsman. While you would be suspect against inswingers if your stance is too side on, you would struggle against away-going deliveries if it is too open. Sachin Tendulkar's is the closest to what would be a perfect stance—though even he tended to lean too much towards the off side when he started.

> The textbook recommends keeping the hands close to each other on the handle, to ensure that they move in unison. Yet Miandad's grip, with hands apart, allowed him to manoeuvre the bowling and milk it for singles.

Even the way you take guard can give the bowler a pointer or two. Generally players who ask for a leg-stump guard are good on the off side, for they try to make room by staying beside the line. And the ones who ask for middle stump are good on the leg side, for their endeavour is to whip it through the leg side. It is not a hard-and-fast rule but any information is better than none at all.

If a batsman is falling over, with his head not in line with his toes—which is the case with a lot of batsmen—he will predominantly be an on-side player, but would still be susceptible to sharp, incoming deliveries. Also, the intended ground shots on the leg side will probably travel in the air for a while and hence positioning a fielder at short midwicket comes in handy. Such a batsman would also be unsure of his off stump and hence might play balls that are meant to be left alone.

The backlift

The last clues before the ball is finally bowled come from the height of the backlift and its arc. Ideally, the bat should come down from somewhere between the off stump and first slip, to ensure that the bat moves straight in the downswing.

Players who bring the bat in from wider than second slip, like Rahul Dravid, need to make a loop at the top of the downswing, or else they will find it difficult to negotiate sharp incoming deliveries. Should they fail to make that loop, the bat won't come down straight, which means meeting the ball at an angle instead of straight on.

Batsmen with higher backlifts find it difficult to deal with changes of pace, because with higher backlifts it is tougher to pull out of a shot after committing. Also, there is always a possibility they will be late in bringing the bat down to keep yorkers out. Ergo, yorkers and slower ones might just do the trick.

Since players with short backlifts—like Paul Collingwood and Andrew Symonds—don't have a reasonable downswing, they rely on the pace of the ball to generate power for their shots. They tend to struggle if the ball has no pace on it; so taking the pace off isn't a bad move against them. On the contrary, short backlifts are almost ideal to keep out yorkers.

If anyone has to think on his feet in cricket, it is the bowler. For it is he who initiates the action and everyone else reacts to what he delivers. Yet, these days he is the game's underdog, constantly at risk of being on the receiving end and bound to follow a plan to render himself effective. Since video data isn't available to teams before they reach a certain level, most bowlers rely on observing the finer nuances of their opponents in order to strategize.

READING THE BOWLER

The replay comes up in slo-mo for us to get a closer look: Brett Lee runs in and bowls a short-pitched delivery at 150 km per hour. Sachin Tendulkar seems to have all the time in the world to get into the right position—he goes back and across and plays it right under his eyes. The pace at which the TV camera reruns it makes it look a cakewalk, an everyday shot, but the batsman gets only a fraction of a second to judge, decide and execute. What is it that enabled the likes of Sachin to tweak their responses and plan their shots?

Let me break it down further for you. At the point of release, a batsman must ascertain the line and length of the delivery, weigh his options with regard to his response (attacking or defensive) and then move quickly to get his body into the right position to execute the option chosen. One of the principles of batting is to be prompt and to be in a position to receive the ball, as against arriving at the same time as the ball, because that is invariably too late. The quicker the bowler, the less time you have in hand to act. If the batsman fails to get his calculations right in time, he is most likely doomed. Unlike against slower bowlers, with whom you may have a second chance.

Judging the line and length

If judging the line and length early makes batting relatively more easy and effective, failure to do so puts the batsman at a disadvantage.

To judge the length, the batsman must watch the point of release of the delivery. The earlier the release, the fuller the ball, which in effect means that if the bowler delivers the ball at the first point of release, it would result in a beamer. Every subsequent delay in release would mean a reduction in the length, with the bouncer being the last point of release. That is the reason every batsman is taught to be ready for the full ball first, because that is the first possibility; if the bowler passes that point of release without delivering, the mind starts sending the body signals to be prepared to go on the back foot.

Batsmen around the world grow up playing bowlers with high-arm actions and hence their minds are attuned to trying to ascertain the length by looking at the point of release. But if you are up against someone like Lasith Malinga or Mitchell Johnson, both of whom have slinging, round-arm actions, it is simply not possible to know the length for sure at the time of the delivery, as there is always a doubt about whether the release was early or delayed. The angle at which the arm comes down leaves a lot to the imagination; unfortunately, though, there isn't much time to imagine at their pace.

Another important aspect that influences the ability to judge length is the position of the batsman's head in his stance. Ideally, the head should be still and the eyes level to be able to judge the length correctly. If the head is tilted upwards, even slightly, all deliveries might seem short-pitched.

Next comes the line. Batsmen try to keep a close eye on

the bowler's wrist at the point of delivery and the position of the wrist with regards to the crease. In case of a fast bowler, the tilt of the wrist may help send the ball in the direction it is tilted towards. When Ishant Sharma's wrist tilts towards the on side, you are more or less sure the ball will swing in to the right hander. This isn't foolproof though, especially when the ball is reverse swinging. Waqar Younis used to keep the wrist completely upright, or even slightly tilted towards the off side, while making the ball dip in to the batsman.

Wrist position is a good giveaway when it comes to reading spinners, many of whom cock their wrists to bowl top-spinners. Similarly, the back of a leg-spinner's hand will usually face the batsman when he tries to bowl a googly. These variations are subtle but if observed and decoded accurately, they can help the batsman.

Makhaya Ntini's wide-of-the-crease action gave away the angle of his stock deliveries, which came in to the right-hander, while Glenn McGrath's close-to-the-stumps action ensured the ball stayed on a well-defined line around the off stump. An off-spinner will usually prefer to come in close to the stumps to bowl the top-spinner (or a floater).

While the wrists and the action will give you clues, keeping a still head in the stance, almost in line with the toes, is vital to your ability to judge line correctly as a batsman. The moment the head starts falling over, the lines get blurred—a problem Rohit Sharma faced quite often in his career. Since his head falls over, he is either chasing balls that should be left alone or finding the ball finishing in line with the front pad instead of in line with the downswing of his bat. From there on, it is just a matter of when and not if he misses one.

Swing and drift

Batsmen also try to look at the way the bowler has gripped the ball, with regards to the position of his fingers and the orientation of the shiny surface. When bowling a slower one McGrath would hold the ball with his index and middle fingers split wide apart; Lee, on the other hand would hold the ball deep in his hand. Zaheer Khan often bowls with his fingers across the seam, which tells you to be ready for a straight delivery because the ball won't swing unless the seam is upright.

> One of the principles of batting is to be prompt and to be in a position to receive the ball, as against arriving at the same time as the ball, because that is invariably too late.

The shiny surface, if visible, often gives away the direction in which the ball will move in the air. For instance, an off-spinner's drift can be read by looking at which way the shiny part of the ball faces. If the ball is swinging conventionally, it will drift into the right-hander if the shiny side is outside, and vice versa. Keeping the shine facing the palm not only takes the ball away in the air, it also makes it skid after pitching, as the ball lands on the shiny side. Obviously, looking at the shine doesn't help much if you're up against the likes of Muralitharan, or someone who prefers to bowl with a scrambled seam.

Leg position

Once the line is deciphered, a batsman will mostly try to keep the front leg inside the line of the ball. For a right-hander the front leg must stay on the leg side of the ball. If the leg is not in the appropriate position, the bat will never come down straight, and you might end up playing across in front of your pads. Also, keeping the leg outside the line is mandatory to maintain good balance, or else you risk falling over.

There is a good chance, though, that these lines will get blurred when the ball is swinging or spinning too much. Murali and Warne have wreaked havoc because batsmen were never sure of the amount of turn off the surface while facing them. What started out seeming the correct place to plant the front foot often proved incorrect in the end. It is the same when the ball is reverse swinging. Haven't we seen Waqar and Wasim hit people on the toes umpteen times?

Things are slightly more manageable on the back foot, because not only does the short ball give a little more time to adjust, it also doesn't swing as much.

The role bounce plays

Tall bowlers with high-arm actions, like McGrath, Ambrose, Kumble and so on, tend to generate more bounce than their round arm, slingy counterparts like Malinga or Ajit Agarkar. While tall bowlers get consistent high bounce, it also often misleads the batsman into playing on the back foot, even to balls that are meant to be played on the front foot; this results in them getting trapped in front. On the other hand, bowlers like Malinga and Agarkar pose a different kind of threat: you can never trust the bounce with them. Playing horizontal bat shots and ducking—for both of which you need to be able to trust the bounce—are difficult while facing these bowlers. You have to tell yourself to be on the front foot, even if the length and pace are pushing you back, and also to play with a vertical bat as much as possible, to make up for the lack of bounce.

Then there is the rare breed of freakish actions, which take a while to make sense of. Remember Paul Adams and how he took the world by storm initially? He was bowling normal chinamen and wrong 'uns but batsmen were hopelessly caught in the flurry of limbs. Such actions are a batsman's nightmare when you are up against them for the first time. Your brain will eventually find ways to look for certain nuances to decode the mystery. That is why it is important for these bowlers to keep evolving, because once the novelty wears off, they become easy pickings.

RUNNING BETWEEN THE WICKETS

When Herschelle Gibbs dropped a catch off Steve Waugh in the 1999 World Cup Super Six match, it felt like he had dropped the cup. Waugh apparently said as much to Gibbs. The slip-up cost South Africa the game, but it was another error that sealed their fate. A horrible mix-up between Lance Klusener and Allan Donald, while attempting the run to win the semi-final, led to Australia's entry into the final.

Batting is not about strokeplay alone; running between the wickets is a crucial part of it. Yet, for a long time it was considered a mediocre player's way of getting the scoreboard ticking; it was believed that the best batsmen preferred to score in boundaries and sixes. Not enough importance was given to this aspect of the game till the shorter version made its presence felt. Unlike five-day cricket, in the limited-overs game captains don't employ attacking fields throughout the day, so taking singles to rotate strike is almost mandatory to keep the scoreboard moving. So much so, that a number of one-day specialists built their games around taking singles: Michael

Bevan, Ajay Jadeja, Robin Singh, to name a few. These were extremely fit men, who took sadistic pleasure in testing the fitness levels of the opposition.

I first learned about the importance of this facet of the game by watching Dean Jones. There may have been others before him who were really good at it, but to my young, impressionable mind, it was Jones who revolutionized running between the wickets. For me, he ticked all the boxes one must to be an efficient runner. That is when I realized that running between the wickets is as much an art as it is a skill.

Backing up

Contrary to popular belief, running between the wickets starts at the non-striker's end. Of course, the striker knows best how hard and how far from the fielder he has hit the ball and, being in motion already, he finds it easy to make a move. While the striker knows, the non-striker assumes and tries to make up for the lack of information by taking a start to gain momentum.

The ideal time for the non-striker to start moving used to be after the bowler lands his back foot in his bowling stride but now, he must wait for the bowler to release the ball, for the rules have changed a little bit about 'mankading'. Therefore, he should back up only to the point from where he can return easily if required. The bat should always be held in the hand closest to the bowler.

Calling

As a kid, I was taught that the striker must call when he has hit the ball in front of the stumps. Everything hit behind the stumps was considered the non-striker's call; the reason being, the non-striker has a good view of a ball hit behind the stumps.

Unfortunately, this is as wrong as it can possibly get. It is natural for the batsman to look in the direction of the shot he has played and hence he is in a better position to know the angles. So, even if the ball goes behind the batsman on strike, it is his call. The non-striker rarely has accurate information. From his vantage point, he can never be certain if the ball is going slightly to the left or right of the fielder or straight to him. The striker knows how much power he put behind the shot, the angles involved and the realistic chance of rotating strike.

But there are moments when the striker can't see the ball at all: when the ball goes to the wicketkeeper and he fumbles, or when the ball hits the striker's pads and he isn't sure where it went. That is when the non-striker must chip in. Also, the non-striker has the right to say no.

Virender Sehwag is the ideal non-striker in this scenario. He is always looking for cheeky singles. He believes that if the keeper has to dive to the side, it is an opportunity to cross over, since the keeper will need time to get up, remove his gloves and throw.

Turning and sliding

Everyone knows that the shortest distance between two points is a straight line, but a lot of batsmen don't follow the rule when turning for a second or third run. Surprisingly, Jonty Rhodes was among these players. Instead of touching down and turning on the spot, he would go around in a small arc at the end. But then he had the speed to make up for it.

If you are not as quick as him, you are better off making a tight turn. And while turning for the second or third run, keep an eye on the ball and make sure you switch the bat from one hand to the other to do this effectively if you need to. A matter of seconds can be the difference between a good run and a run-out. Turning blind costs you those micro-seconds.

Jones impressed me with the way he ran only as much as he absolutely needed to. He would hold the bat high on the handle so as to use its length to the optimum, and while turning he would stay low and stretch fully. While staying low helped him generate the necessary thrust to turn quickly and gain momentum again, stretching the arms and the body allowed him to run at least one step fewer.

Everyone knows you should always slide the bat into the crease, but it is important to remember to slide either the face or the edge of the bat. Earlier, coaches believed it was best to use only the edge, but considering the bat sometimes gets stuck that way, the approach has changed. Another benefit of having the bat face the ground is that when you dive to make the crease, the bat stays grounded. If you try diving in with the back of the bat facing down, the curve of the blade sometimes leaves vital inches of the bat in the air.

Also, one must not forget the importance of staying off the business area of the pitch at all times. The only exception to this rule used to be when you had to come in the way of a throw to avoid getting run out which is not allowed anymore, for if a batsman changes his natural path of running and causes obstruction to the trajectory of the ball, he will be considered out even if the ball doesn't hit the stumps.

Judgement, rapport, strategy

Speed is overrated in running between wickets. Yes, you need to be quick to get to the other end but a good sprinter may not necessarily be a good runner between wickets. It is more about your awareness and judgement with regard to the power with which you have hit the ball, and the ability of the fielder.

But it always starts with the intent. Both Gautam Gambhir and Sehwag were good examples here—though, while you have to give them full marks for intent, their judgement can be questioned at times. The person who rarely got it wrong in judging was Sachin Tendulkar. Invariably he knew how many runs are available right from the moment he hit the ball. You rarely saw him huffing and puffing or diving to make his ground.

In many instances there are only one-and-a-half or two-and-a-half runs available. That is when good runners put pressure on the fielder. M.S. Dhoni is excellent at this. He is extremely quick between the wickets and uses that speed to steal an extra run whenever possible.

Since calling is based on judgement, the moment it isn't spot-on, you are in a dilemma. At times, the striker takes the non-striker's running skills into account before calling for a run, which invariably leads to disaster.

Misunderstandings also occur often, especially in loud and noisy stadia. It is almost impossible to hear each other through the din, so one reacts on instinct and based on faith in one's partner. This is where knowing the other person well helps. No wonder Gauti and Viru were good friends off the field too.

Good runners either know or decide in advance the path each will be taking while running. Ideally the striker should run down the off-side channel and the non-striker on the leg side, but it changes if the bowler goes around the stumps or if a left-hander bowls over the stumps to a right-hand batsman or vice versa. In such cases it is the non-striker who gives way to the striker and runs further away from the stumps.

Dealing with a substitute runner is also a challenge. The rule here is that it is always the striker's call and the substitute must not assume anything but only react to the call and respond appropriately. Problems happen when the substitute starts calling from square leg and the non-striker doesn't know where to look.

Running as a weapon

Stealing a single right under the nose of a fielder, especially a good one, is a kick. At times you push the envelope too much, test a good fielder, punt and fall short. Sehwag, though a good runner, is often guilty of running himself out, even in Test matches.

Both he and I took a lot of pride in running the Australians tired in the 2003-04 series. We hadn't decided beforehand that taking singles would be the strategy to ruffle them. Viru is always eager to get on and off strike, and for me, singles were a lifeline against disciplined bowling.

It started when we ran a single in the first Test in Brisbane. The fielder at gully threw a lobbed ball to the man at point. Since the ball hadn't reached the keeper, it wasn't dead. We sensed an opportunity and ran.

There is nothing a bowler hates more than leaking singles. He doesn't mind getting hit for fours because he knows he bowled a bad ball, but going for runs on good balls irks him big time. Also, if the strike is rotated, it means he has to bowl to a different batsman each time, which means he can't plan a dismissal.

You need to be a little cheeky too. I remember Ajay Jadeja once running when the striker was caught at slip off a no-ball. The fielder threw the ball in the air to celebrate without realizing it was a no-ball. Jadeja was more aware and stole a single.

With the margin of victory getting smaller in the shorter formats, and captains opting for defensive field positions in Test cricket, running between the wickets has become ever so crucial.

SECTION TWO

THE ART AND CRAFT

THE ART OF CAPTAINCY

Was it really the captaincy of Shane Warne that drove the Rajasthan Royals to the title in the first edition of the Indian Premier League (IPL)? If yes, Royal Challengers Bangalore's change in fortunes and run-up to the top spot in IPL-2 probably had much to do with Kevin Pietersen making way for Anil Kumble. Chennai Super Kings' consistent form over the last seven years must have something to do with their charismatic leader—M.S. Dhoni. And Pietersen's second innings' failure with Delhi Daredevils must say something about his leadership skills, or the lack of them.

People watch the IPL from different vantage points; among other things, I often make it a point to look at the nuances in the leadership styles of different captains.

Some think captaincy is the most overrated aspect in this format, while others believe it is what makes the difference in the end. For me, the captain is as good as his team, but I don't rule out the impact he can have on the final upshot. A captain may not be able to win with a very poor side, but he can always make a team punch above its weight.

Leadership by example

Some mistake this sort of captaincy with just performance on the field, but there is more to it. The captain's conduct is the easiest way to send a message across. If a captain is disciplined, like Rahul Dravid or Ricky Ponting—their work ethic is immaculate—the team follows suit automatically. You'll see both Dravid and Ponting do fielding drills even after a long training session, and that is signal enough for others to go the extra mile. Perhaps the one-handed catch Ponting took at cover for the Mumbai Indians in IPL-6 wouldn't have been possible without those extra drills.

On the contrary, since Warne thinks that warming up before a match is not a very useful exercise, his team stayed away from it in the second edition of the IPL. While it worked for Warne, others found it difficult to play without and perhaps the results reflected that.

One can also not discount the importance of an in-form captain. Once his game is taken care of, a captain can allow his focus to shift to other issues. Alastair Cook's extended lack of form for England might have been a reason for them not turning the tide sooner.

Leadership by direction

Captains use this form of leadership on newcomers, who need to be given instructions, depending on the situation of the game and the player's role in the team. That is exactly what happened when I played for India: I was told about my role in no uncertain terms and there was no room for negotiation. One may think this sort of thing may be a hindrance in the growth of a player but the exact opposite is true. It prepares a player to adapt to the different demands of the game and hence makes him better in the long run. You're taught right at the beginning to put the team ahead of yourself. If the need of the hour is to occupy the crease and build a partnership, you must put your head down and resist the temptation to be adventurous. Similarly, if you need to throw caution to the winds in the slog overs, you should not think twice about sacrificing your wicket.

Leadership by seduction

This form of leadership works with players who've started to find their feet but still haven't made it. You dangle a carrot to get the best out of them. You set targets for them and if they achieve those, you reward them in return. For example, asking the likes of Ajinkya Rahane and Rohit Sharma to be more consistent while batting at five or six and rewarding them by promoting them up the batting order after a while. You do such things with people who you genuinely believe have talent and need some encouragement to fulfil their potential.

Leadership by association

Once a player is comfortable with his game and knows most of what needs to be done, the captain makes him a part of the decision-making process. They discuss strategies and make

> As a player, if I know that my captain is going to stand by me, I'll happily stretch that extra bit. But if I'm not sure, like I personally wasn't with Brendon McCullum for Kolkata last year, I'd hold back. Why would a player do anything for a captain who doesn't even remember his name?

plans together. The captain asks the player for his opinion and instead of giving orders makes suggestions. This is the sort of method Dhoni was probably employing with Zaheer Khan: he had faith in Zaheer's ability and knew that he didn't need every last detail spelt out for him. So they formed a partnership of sorts, where both gave inputs and the captain got things done.

Leadership by delegation

There comes a time when a player is so experienced, he doesn't need to be told what to do. He knows what works best for him and no amount of persuasion will make him think otherwise. To get the best from such a cricketer, the captain must respect his experience and allow him to do whatever he is comfortable with. If he is at his best, batting a certain way or bowling to a certain field, the captain should allow that to happen as long as it is not ruining the team's chances of winning. In turn, the player acknowledges that freedom and rarely lets the captain or team down. The art here is to get someone to do something you want done because he wants to do it. This is probably the sort of leadership Dravid must have employed with Rahane for the Rajasthan Royals. Rahane was given the freedom to bat at his own pace (though obviously not too slow), while others around him complemented his efforts by going after the bowling.

A captain must understand that good communication is the key. It is imperative for him to be available to every single player and be able to talk to them in a language they understand. It becomes even more important while leading an IPL team because the players are from different parts of the world, with different temperaments and backgrounds. A captain needs to go the extra yard to understand what makes them tick and how to handle each of them.

As a player, if I know that my captain is going to stand by me, I'll happily stretch that extra bit. But if I'm not sure—like I personally wasn't with Brendon McCullum for Kolkata Knight Riders in the second season of the IPL—I'd hold myself back. Why would a player do anything for a captain who doesn't even remember his name? Pietersen apparently forgot the names of his Royal Challengers teammates. No wonder things changed when Kumble took over.

As a captain you have to be one of the players yet maintain an aura that commands respect. You must create an environment in which a player feels secure of his place in the side and let him express himself both on the ground and off it. A player should also know that his captain will support him to the hilt. The same McCullum who struggled for Kolkata Knight Riders became the inspirational leader for New Zealand in their successful 2015 World Cup campaign and the team emulated his fiery brand of cricket.

Sounds a lot of work, right? And we haven't even touched upon the skills required to make bowling changes, make and execute plans and all the rest of it. A captain certainly has a lot on his plate.

I'm reminded of a beautiful quote by John Quincy Adams: 'If your actions inspire others to dream more, learn more, do more and become more, you are a leader.'

The next time you watch a captain walk away with the honours, spend a moment thinking of the ordeal he has gone through to get there.

ADVANTAGE LEFTIES

Don't you think left-hand batsmen look more elegant? Aren't effective left-arm spinners easier to find, as opposed to a quality right-arm off-spinners? And don't left-arm seam bowlers have much more to offer than their right-arm counterparts? What is it about lefties that is so right? What is it that makes them ever so exhilarating to watch in action?

Left-arm quick bowlers

When you're facing a left-arm seamer bowling from over the wicket, if you're a right-hand batsman, you immediately have to open up your stance a bit, from the toes to the upper body, to have a complete view of the bowler and the path of the ball. It is one of the few instances in cricket when you are advised not to stay side-on, for if you remain completely side-on, you'll only be able to see the bowler from the corner of your eye, and that would impair your judgement. So, even before he has bowled a ball, the bowler has forced the batsman to make an adjustment.

Left-arm seamers also have a flair for making the straight ball look like it has done something when it slants across to a batsman. It is just the angle taking the ball away from the right-hander, but from twenty-two yards away it feels like it is going away rather than just travelling in a straight line. In such conditions, the batsman can always do with a bit of extra bounce, as there was when India played in Australia in 2003-04. Nathan Bracken and India's left-arm bowlers consistently made the ball hold its line, and even dart back in, but as a batsman you could always trust the bounce to take it over the top of the stumps if you misread an inswinger for a straight one.

Also, you can live with the ball that slants across, as the leg-before option is ruled out. If a ball of this sort is going on to hit the stumps, it invariably pitches outside leg stump; and if it pitches in line, the angle takes it away from the stumps.

When Zaheer Khan started playing for India, he was a prime example of a left-arm bowler who slanted the ball across. Despite being quicker, he was relatively easier to play then than he is now. Both Virender Sehwag and I had played him in a Duleep Trophy game. While the angle allowed me to leave everything that pitched even on off stump, it provided enough width for Viru to unleash his square cuts.

But as soon as the ball starts swinging in to the right-hander, in the air and off the surface, a host of new possibilities open up. As a batsman, your first instinct is to get the pad out of the way, because the leg-before is a left-arm swing bowler's bread-and-butter dismissal. So you tend to play inside the line, and sometimes even with a short stride forward, to ensure that you play with the bat.

It is easier to go a lot more forward, and probably outside the line, to a right-arm inswing bowler, but you can't do that with a left-armer for two reasons. One: since you're standing with your stance open, it is almost impossible to go that far across. Two, and more importantly, the natural swing tends to finish within the stumps because of the angle the ball is bowled from. A right-arm inswing bowler tends to bowl from wider of the crease and the angle takes the ball down the leg side, but that is not the case with the left-arm bowler. Swing and seam movement allow him to pitch it outside the off stump. Sometimes it shapes back in and on other occasions it just holds its line. Both can be dangerous. Under normal circumstances, if the ball is pitched a fair bit outside the off stump, it doesn't come in enough after pitching to pose a threat. It is a fine line, though. An inch either way can make the difference.

Left-arm bowlers have another weapon in their armoury. When the ball gets old, they come from around the wicket and make the batsman's job even more difficult. Since outswingers are a rarity with the old ball, the batsman can always make the adjustment of staying inside the line. But the dynamics change while facing a left-arm quick, for he can take the ball away from a right-hand batsman. Also, the angle at which they deliver makes you play at the ball.

Spinners at a glance

Can you imagine a right-arm off-spinner surviving in this day and age without slightly bending his arm and without bowling a doosra? I doubt it. But you can if you're a left-arm spinner. The mere fact that they take the ball away from the right-hand batsman makes them worthy of a place in the side, while a right-hand off-spinner in contrast must have plenty of tricks to keep the batsman quiet—because it is always easier to hit the ball spinning in to the batsman. Not only are the chances of getting stumped fewer with off breaks, it is ideal for the batsman's natural swing, which is to go over long on and midwicket. Of course, slow left-armers face the same predicament while bowling to left-hand batsmen, but there aren't too many of the latter around.

Left-hand batsmen

One might perhaps assume that right-arm bowlers enjoy the same advantages against left-hand batsmen that left-armers do against right-hand batsmen, but nothing could be farther from the truth. There are only a handful of bowlers, like Glenn McGrath, who have felt comfortable bowling to left-hand batsmen.

In theory, bowlers like Muttiah Muralitharan and Harbhajan Singh should love being able to take the ball away from left-hand batsmen, but even they prefer to bowl at right-hand batsmen.

It is all about practice and the more you bowl at certain types of batsmen, the better you become at it. When you're almost always bowling to right-handers, you develop a line that is suitable to counter them. That is why both Harbhajan and Muralitharan were reluctant to go around the stumps while bowling to southpaws. But by bowling from over the wicket, you almost rule out the lbw, because either the ball pitches outside the line of the leg stump, or if it pitches in line, it misses the stumps. Only a doosra, or a floater pitching in line with the stumps, can get the batsman leg-before from that angle.

The same applies for the right-arm quicks against left-hand batsmen. If they stay over the wicket, the only way to get a leg-before decision is to get close to the stumps, start swinging the ball in from outside the off stump (which they aren't used to) and then finish in line with the stumps. If they go around the wicket, they go wide on the crease and the angle takes the ball down the leg side. If getting a leg-before is tough from over the wicket, it is ever tougher from around the wicket.

But even left-hand batsmen have a small handicap to deal with: the rough created by right-arm bowlers. Since there usually are more right-armers around, there is more damage on the side of the pitch that happens to be the area just outside off stump for a left-hander. But that is a small price to pay for other major benefits.

Researchers at Oxford University believe they have found a gene that increases the odds of being left-handed. Certainly, if a way is ever found of manufacturing this gene, every cricket-obsessed parent who wants his kid to play cricket would be a potential customer. I, too, would perhaps give my right hand for an ingenious left hand—much like tennis champion Rafael Nadal, whose uncle made sure his nephew made his left his right.

BALL TAMPERING

The ball-biting incident involving Shahid Afridi, perhaps the most bizarre instance of ball tampering, had created quite a furore in international cricket. It was extremely silly of Shahid Afridi to believe he could get away with an outlandish act like that, considering the number of cameras covering the game. He was caught red-handed and slapped with a two-match ban, which some thought was a rap on the knuckles for someone with a bit of a history. Remember how he danced on the pitch during a break in the Faisalabad Test against England in 2005?

So, what is it that incites a bowler to meddle with the ball? Certainly not just a flash of unscrupulousness. Even men of character like Sachin Tendulkar and Rahul Dravid have been reprimanded for ball tampering.

Cricket, right from its inception, has by and large been a batsman's game. To add to the bowler's woes, the game's rules have been mended over the years to further the interests of batsmen. Bats have become better, grounds smaller and tracks flatter. Right from discouraging bodyline bowling—by not allowing more than two fielders between the square-leg umpire and the wicketkeeper—, limiting the number of bouncers, imposing fielding restrictions for the first fifteen overs—this now includes a batting powerplay as well—, cricket has become overwhelmingly batsman friendly.

Some might argue that all this has actually increased bowlers' market value, because good bowlers are worth their weight in gold now. The IPL auctions over the years seemed to bear this in mind: Dale Steyn, Lasith Malinga, Sunil Narine aren't even allowed to get to the auction table and hence it is only fair to assume that they went for big money. Be that as it may, these days, quality bowling doesn't always translate into performance on the field, thanks to the way the odds are stacked heavily against bowlers, especially in the shorter formats; most bowlers, regardless of talent, go for plenty. Taking a beating in the park may not be denting their bank accounts but it definitely is bruising their ego and self-respect.

I remember being introduced to ball tampering during my debut first-class season, nearly two decades ago. Our bowlers were getting alarming movement in the air and off the surface. The ball was rather new (and a new SG ball doesn't move that much), the track was a typical Kotla one, a batting beauty, and it was the third morning; so there was no day-one moisture.

I wasn't playing the game but sitting on the sidelines admiring the quality of bowling on display. When I went in to field as a substitute I noticed that our bowlers had tinkered with the ball. One side was still shiny and even had the manufacturer's stamp, while the other side was completely scuffed up. Of course they had worked on it beyond imagination, using bottle caps or something equally sharp. I was surprised on two counts: that both umpires didn't notice the manipulation despite wickets falling at regular intervals (considering umpires get the ball at the fall of every wicket), and that the batting side remained unfazed and didn't complain. In those days though, umpires didn't have so much power, or maybe they didn't exercise it as much.

Since then, I have realized that ball tampering does not happen randomly. It is, more often than not, part of the game plan. Some do it discreetly, while the rest, like Afridi, are either brave or foolish enough to do it blatantly. Some even say it is a craft and by that logic, I have witnessed a few craftsmen at work in my career. The use of nails, especially thumbnails, comes in handy. One cricketer used to do it so subtly that you wouldn't come to know even if you were standing next to him while he did so. We even challenged him to do it while talking to the umpire once, and he pulled it off, like a pro.

Most teams and bowlers around the world lift the seam. It can be done so subtly that umpires and cameras will never catch the offender.

I have realized that ball tampering does not happen randomly. It is more often than not part of the game plan.

Then there are ways known only to a few people. A bowling legend from a neighbouring country once said that it takes only a few overs to make the ball reverse-swing. He wouldn't tell us the tricks of the trade but he didn't deny that he was an able practitioner of the craft.

I don't know of teams who aren't aware of the effectiveness of sugar-laden saliva. Rahul Dravid was reprimanded once because he accidentally dropped a half-eaten sweet on the ball, but most players do so intentionally.

There was even a case of Vaseline coming to the rescue in a domestic game. This was a few years ago when there was a batch of SG Test balls that wouldn't shine regardless of the work one put in. Even mints were ineffective; so Vaseline became the last resort. It worked, but only just.

There are other absolutely legitimate ways of scuffing up the ball. Instead of bowling seam-up, fast bowlers can bowl cross-seam. While you can never be completely sure of landing the ball on the surface that is already scuffed up, this method is effective at the beginning, when you're deciding which side to shine. Throwing the ball one-bounce in from the outfield is another way of ensuring that the scuffed-up surface gets abraded more when it hits the ground. And unlike while bowling, you can ensure that it lands on the rough side every time.

It is basic human nature to look for ways to survive. I'm not defending the practice of ball tampering; I'm merely drawing attention towards its causes. Since this game is at its best when the competition between the bat and ball is fair, we must ensure that it is attained without resorting to any unfair practice.

But bowlers will need support. For starters, you need to prepare tracks that have something in them for seamers and spinners. Then, we may need to mend a few rules to make bowlers feel that their role is a bit more than just feeding batsmen balls to be hit. For example, in ODIs, fast bowlers used to bank on the ball getting old and producing reverse-swing towards the end of an innings. That opportunity was taken away from them when the ball was changed at the completion of the thirty-fourth over, and if that wasn't enough to render reverse swing useless, the current ODI regulations have two new balls in the game, one from each end. Good luck to you if you're banking on getting some reverse swing with the old ball, for even in the fiftieth over, the ball is just twenty-five overs old.

One could also allow three fielders outside the circle in the first powerplay and be slightly lenient when it came to wides, especially leg-side ones. Only balls that can't be hit should be adjudged wides, unlike the present rule where anything down the leg side is a wide. A no-ball is followed by a free-hit. When batsmen don't get penalized for mistiming a shot or getting beaten, why are we so severe on bowlers for overstepping the crease or for a slight error in line? Give bowlers some room for error, and perhaps allow them to use mints to shine the ball—which, in any case, most teams are already doing. Yet, at the same time, have stricter penalties for tampering the ball using teeth, bottle caps, spikes or non-permissible objects.

PLAYING ON BOUNCY WICKETS

India's tour to England in 2014 was a good example of how the nature of pitches can change the way cricket is played during the match. I firmly believe that the quality of cricket produced in a match is directly proportional to the quality of pitch prepared for the game. It didn't surprise anyone that the pitch at Trent Bridge for the first Test match was deemed 'poor' by the match-referee David Boon, for it was an uneven contest between the bat and ball. On the contrary, the pitch at Old Trafford was the best pitch in the series. The key difference between two surfaces was bounce, which Old Trafford had in abundance. At Trent Bridge even when the batsman nicked while driving, the ball didn't carry to the slip cordon; meanwhile at Old Trafford, a poke was enough to put the ball in the slip fielder's lap.

The two extremes do exist. In my opinion, bounce is the key factor in the quality of a track. It is the bounce that makes stroke-making easy and the lack of it that makes batting predictable.

The low blows

You are more likely to find low-bounce surfaces in the

subcontinent and, perhaps, in the West Indies these days. In theory, all you need to do on such surfaces is stay on the front foot and play with a straight bat. In practice though, it is quite difficult to take a long stride forward when the ball is pitched short, especially when the bowler at the other end is Shoaib Akhtar.

I remember watching Shoaib bowl at full throttle on a low Kotla pitch. He was bowling in the high 140s and getting the ball to reverse swing too. There are only a few batsmen in the world who can take a long stride forward to a genuinely quick bowler, let alone stretch forward when the ball is pitched short. Fortunately during that match, we had one such batsman, Rahul Dravid, but even he found the low bounce difficult to negotiate. He went forward on almost every occasion, but still couldn't stop one from breaching his defence.

Similar scenes were repeated in the Champions League matches played in Delhi. Even though the mind tells you to get forward when Brett Lee has bowled short of a good length, the body simply refuses to go forward. It is sort of a reflex action.

Bowlers are smart operators and aren't shy of banging it in short on a regular basis on such surfaces. Since you can never be sure of the bounce, it isn't advisable to duck underneath the ball, but getting on top of every bouncer is not possible either, even when the wicket is keeping low.

In the first Test at Trent Bridge, a lot of batsmen got hit on the body because of the lack of bounce. Pitching on the exact same length, some deliveries sailed comfortably over the head and some had the batsmen in a tangle. Ideally, you should try to play every short-pitched ball and then either get on top of it or sway away.

It is important for the batsman to remember not to be impulsive. A good puller of the ball, for instance, automatically sets himself up for a pull as soon as the ball is dropped short. Ricky Ponting had first-hand experience of this in a warm-up game in Hyderabad some years ago. Irfan Pathan kept banging the ball in short and Ponting kept playing horizontal shots and kept turning around to see the ball bounce twice before reaching the wicketkeeper. Every time he did it, I asked him if he was enjoying the bounce.

Later in the match, I too fell victim to the lack of bounce. I went back and across to a Stuart Clark bouncer and expected to play the ball around my ribs, but to my utter disbelief the ball crashed into my shoes. This time it was Ponting ribbing me about the bounce.

On such surfaces, the fielders standing in the slips, along with the wicketkeeper, suffer as much as the batsmen. Many times you might have criticized the keeper and the fielder at first-slip for letting a few go between them, but on pitches with low bounce you hardly get the time to react. The pace at which a bowler bowls isn't reduced, but fielders have to come up a long way to ensure that edges carry to them. While you stand almost at the thirty-yard circle in Australia, at times you have to stand at not more than 15 yards away to the same bowler on low tracks. Good fielders keep coming up because it is better to drop a catch on the full—at least you have a chance to catch it—than watch the ball land in front of you.

The high tide

While playing on surfaces with extra bounce, a batsman needs to stay on the back foot and play with the horizontal bat more often. Even though it is tougher to adjust to high bounce than low bounce, it is still manageable.

The problem is when the bounce is unpredictable. The West Indies attack posed all kinds of problems to the Australian batting in South Africa during the Champions Trophy in 2008. The ball was bouncing alarmingly from a good length to hit Ponting and friends on the hands or other parts of their bodies.

All you can do on such surfaces is have decisive footwork—which Ponting did have on that day—and try and get to the pitch of the ball whenever it is pitched up and use the depth of the crease to go fully back when pitched short.

On such surfaces, balls pitched fuller cause problems, because there is very little time to adjust to the uneven bounce. Hence bowlers try to keep it up to the bat as much as possible. The batsman needs to counterattack to force a bowler to change his length. That is the reason one goes hard at balls that are pitched up, hoping that the bowler starts bowling short to cut down on the runs conceded. So it isn't always right to criticize a batsman for playing what seems like a reckless shot, because it may just be an attempt to survive.

While most batsmen will not believe or accept it, there are times when one gets scared of uneven bounce. I have seen batsmen, especially in the lower order, back away towards square leg when that happens, and you can't blame them. The match I'm referring to here is a Ranji Trophy game played on an underprepared green top at the Kotla, between Delhi and Orissa. Balls pitched just short of a good length were frequently sailing over the batsman's and wicketkeeper's heads. You not only need a lot of courage but also a big slice of luck to survive on such surfaces.

While batting on surfaces with low bounce isn't dangerous,

it makes for boring cricket beyond a point. On the contrary, it is quite entertaining to see batsmen hopping and jumping while batting on surfaces with uneven bounce on the higher side. But how can one not feel for the batsmen?

BOWLING ON DEAD TRACKS

Some of the tracks laid out in the subcontinent are batting havens—classic 'win-the-toss-bat-first' surfaces—which in most cases, push the team losing the toss into playing catch up for the duration of the match.

On these featherbeds the ball refuses to change its path after pitching, for spinners and fast bowlers alike, and the odds are stacked heavily against the bowlers and the fielding side. But there is a job to be done: to dismiss the opposition, failing which you need to brace yourself for a dreadfully long haul. Nothing hurts a player more than the feeling of helplessness against the inevitable, which in this case is the declaration from the batting side.

Does this mean one resigns to fate and does not plan at all? Definitely not. In fact, bowling on such tracks might need more planning than on helpful surfaces. But planning alone is often not enough; it needs to be complemented with lots of perseverance.

Fast bowlers with the new ball

A fast bowler's planning depends on the ball being used in the match. If the match is in India, it is the SG Test ball that is used, which of course behaves quite differently than the Kookaburra.

The SG ball moves negligibly in the air while it is new, and so it is important to hit the deck hard till one side gets rough. You often see Zaheer Khan bowl cross-seam deliveries right at the beginning of a spell to hasten this process. And I vividly remember Glenn McGrath employing similar tactics in the 2004 series in India.

Unless the team has three seamers at their disposal, it isn't a bad idea to hold back the two frontline quicks till one side of the ball loses its sheen. A part-time quick or a spinner comes handy in these conditions. This was the job Angelo Mathews did for Sri Lanka in India a few years ago.

Once the ball starts swinging, releasing it right, instead of hitting the deck hard, becomes the mantra. The track might not offer lateral movement but the ball will most likely swing in the air, if delivered properly. Since this swing may not be complemented by movement off the surface, field placements may still need to be a little conservative. The bowlers must stick to a line, set their fields accordingly and err only on the side of fullness, for balls pitched short won't even move in the air.

Bowlers must employ different tactics while bowling with the Kookaburra, which, unlike the SG ball, moves appreciably when it is new. Hence the endeavour should be to release the ball properly, pitch it slightly fuller and extract movement in the air. Smart bowlers use the more pronounced seam to bowl cutters too.

Lasith Malinga did something remarkable in the first Test

match against India in Galle (2009). He bowled fuller to start with, dismissed Gautam Gambhir cheaply in both innings and then used the hardness of the ball to push Virender Sehwag on to the back foot with a barrage of well directed bouncers when he saw there wasn't much swing on offer. He knew that once the ball lost its hardness, he would have to wait for it to start reverse-swinging to inflict damage. The trick is to assess the conditions quickly and then react appropriately, be it the SG or the Kookaburra.

Fast bowlers when the ball gets old

The brand of ball makes very little difference in the approach when the ball gets old, when there isn't much conventional swing, no movement off the surface and it is too early to get reverse swing going. That is when discipline and patience take centre stage.

Zaheer was a master operator in these situations, especially in post-lunch sessions in the subcontinent. He bowled at about 70 per cent of his optimum speed, stuck to a line a foot outside off stump, employed a 6–3 or 7–2 off-side field and waited for the batsman to commit harakiri. He had the advantage of the natural angle working for him, taking the ball away from the right-hander even when it wasn't swinging.

Another tactic, if executed well, is to accept that there isn't enough movement to find the outside edge and that even if you do, it is unlikely to carry to the slips. Then one must bowl wicket to wicket, keep the catching fielders in front of the stumps and hope to either breach the defence or expect the batsman to get carried away and hit in the air. You need to be persistent rather than imaginative to see through such phases. But consistency in line and length is imperative, else you'll be punished, for the margin of error is really small. The only thing you must constantly vary is the pace. Rolling your fingers over the ball to bowl slower ones and cutters are among the few ways to create doubt in the batsman's mind in these conditions.

Another tactic is to get two fast bowlers to bowl bouncers in tandem from around the stumps, with both fine leg and square leg on the fence. Since there is nothing happening otherwise, there is no harm in trying something different.

Once the ball starts reverse-swinging, good quick bowlers come into their own. One is still required to stick to a line (you don't want to bowl on both sides of the wicket) but lengths can, and perhaps must, vary with almost every delivery. The last thing you as a bowler want when the ball is reverse swinging is to be predictable. Even a toe-crushing yorker doesn't have the same effect if every ball is in the block-hole.

Once again, Malinga used the old ball quite effectively in the first Test match (2009) to break the back of the Indian batting line-up, dismissing Rahul Dravid, Sachin Tendulkar and M.S. Dhoni. Michael Kasprowicz did something similar in the series against India in 2004. He was so ruthless with his lines around the middle and leg stumps that he could do without a slip or a gully fielder.

While talking about masters with the old ball, it would be criminal not to mention Waqar Younis and Wasim Akram. But these two were special bowlers with special skills and others can only dream of emulating them. Don't they say: planning and plotting is for lesser mortals; geniuses carve their own road?

Spinners

Slow bowlers are your workhorses on dead surfaces, for good captains rarely give their fast bowlers long spells. Spinners are required to do the donkey's work of bowling extremely long spells with or, mostly, without any assistance from the surface. They need strategies too, but unlike for their quicker counterparts, their plans don't vary from Kookaburra to SG, for balls don't behave radically differently depending on their brand when in the hands of a spinner.

Length is not negotiable: they must stick to it for as long as they are bowling or pay for it dearly. The lines and the pace, though, must keep changing, along with the introduction of variations like the doosra, googly or the arm ball.

The lack of purchase from the surface, unless you are a Murali or Warne, might make a spinner monotonous and that is what they must guard against. They must keep using the drift, experiment with angles by coming over and around the stumps, coming close or going away from the stumps and use fielders cleverly to play with the batsman's mind. There may be nothing happening but the batsman must always get the impression that there is a plan in place. And the most likely way for a spinner to get a wicket on these surfaces is to put pressure on the batsman by making run scoring difficult and thus making him commit a faux pas.

I really like how Daniel Vettori operated on good surfaces against quality players of spin bowling. He tried to block their working areas—behind square leg for a left-hander and point for a right-hander—by altering his line and length and placing a fielder to cut off the single. By doing so, he challenged the batsman to do something different, like go over the top or play against the spin. He may not have always been successful, though he mostly was, but his intentions were absolutely right.

In batting-friendly conditions it helps to have a multi-dimensional attack: a couple of attacking bowlers who are expected to aim for wickets—though they might be a little expensive in the bargain—along with a couple of defensive bowlers who will stem the flow of runs and also give their more aggressive counterparts some respite.

Ideally, one would always have tracks like the ones England dished out for the Pakistan–Australia Test series (2004), which had enough in them to keep the bowlers interested. But expecting them from curators in the subcontinent would be a bit too optimistic. While I have written about how a bowler can plan, it is still a bloody tough job to be a bowler in the subcontinent. Unless we make a conscious effort to prepare sporting wickets, it may well cut a few careers short, either due to injury or lack of results. To those who are still standing and delivering in these inhuman conditions: take a bow!

CHANGING ROLES OF AN OPENER

How is Sunil Gavaskar different from Sachin Tendulkar? Or Virender Sehwag from Sourav Ganguly? Or Matthew Hayden from Adam Gilchrist? They are all openers, but is there a difference at all between them? Well, yes and no.

These men are the first to step on the field, the first to face the new ball and mostly, the first to get dismissed in an innings. They have all led the team from the front. Yet, when viewed closely, each displays a distinct individuality, thanks to the difference in the formats they open in.

Opening in Test cricket

It wouldn't be extravagant to propose that opening the batting in Test cricket can be divided into two eras: pre- and post-Sehwag. Despite opening with Viru, I belong to the era before him.

There are certain traits a school coach looks for in a kid before entrusting him with the task of opening the batting. It goes without saying that the batsman ought to be comfortable against pace and swing. Yet it takes much more than just getting into the second line or playing late to succeed at the top.

An opener should be extremely wary of every ball bowled at him. When the new ball is bowled with an upright seam, even if it is travelling straight in the air, he must not treat it as a straight ball because there is always a possibility of it swinging late in the air or moving sideways after pitching. Playing through the line is a complete no-no.

Even as most players' eyes light up at a juicy half-volley, an opener should always tread with caution. Good openers prefer the check-drive over a full-flowing drive for a couple of reasons: firstly, once committed to a drive, it is very difficult to pull out, which you must if the ball moves late; secondly, an opener can time the ball to get maximum rewards. He doesn't need to knock the leather off it.

The same cautious nature takes precedence when it comes to turning the bat inwards while playing off the legs. You wait till the very last moment, right till the point of contact, to turn the wrists because you can never be sure whether the seam, on gripping the surface, will change direction and force a top edge.

That doesn't mean an opener should subdue his instincts completely. He must trust his judgement with regard to how much the ball will swing in the air and deviate after pitching. Else it would be next to impossible to play it. There are no surefire methods of knowing the amount of deviation and hence you must fall back on your experience and gut feeling.

So there are two approaches, both at odds with each other and yet a good opener in Test cricket must have a healthy mix of both to succeed.

The contradiction doesn't end there. Former English cricketer Michael Atherton once told me that an opener must concede that he can't be a perfectionist but still must try to get as close as possible to being perfect.

Since the ball is new, the bowler fresh and the track untested, there will always be deliveries that will defeat you. The trick is to not think about them and to start focusing on the next ball. While it is fine to get beaten every now and then, it is still mandatory that you work towards getting your technique watertight.

A little push down the ground, off both feet, working the ball on the leg side and an occasional square cut were the only ways known to traditional openers for scoring runs early in the innings in Test cricket. Even the square cut wasn't considered a straightforward shot because one must not hit the ball that is still rising. The square cut was only to be played to deliveries that were hittable even after they had acquired the optimum height.

As Sunil Gavaskar would often say, 'Give the first half an hour to the bowler, the remaining five and a half hours are yours,' which means, gauge the bounce and pace of the pitch and try to play as little as possible in the beginning.

There were a few rebels, like Michael Slater, who challenged that school of thought, but no one changed the way opening was perceived as much as Sehwag. He not only scored a lot of runs consistently but also in all conditions.

Now if you want to bat in the Sehwag mould, there is no need to be extra cautious as an opener. You can not only play through the line but also on the up, as long as you hit it regularly. No longer is it mandatory to get on top of the ball to play the square cut, because getting under the ball and hitting it over the gully and slip cordon is also an acceptable shot and a rewarding one as well. Sehwag's batting is a lot about courage of conviction and simple technique. He is extremely successful but you must emulate him at your own peril.

To be fair on the likes of Sehwag and Tillakaratne Dilshan,

the role of an opener in Test cricket has also changed over the years. An opener is no longer expected to see off the shine to shield the No. 4, the best batsman in the team, but instead lead the attack from the front.

Opening in fifty-over cricket

Opening in the shorter format is not as demanding as opening in Test cricket. There is about twice as much room for error in an ODI as compared to Test cricket, for while the ball is moving there are usually two slips at most, maybe the odd gully and no close-in fielders on the leg side.

That is perhaps why we see so many players who would never open the innings in the longer format successfully do so in ODIs. In fact, opening is considered the best position to bat in the shorter format because not only do you get to bat the most overs, you also enjoy the first powerplay. And unlike in T20, here you can play a few quiet overs to get your eye in.

Opening in the fifty-over version follows a regimented routine for most: play the new white ball with caution and then change gears as the game progresses. It is almost mandatory to keep hitting boundaries at regular intervals to keep the scoreboard moving, because stealing singles with nine men inside the ring isn't easy. For instance, though Gautam Gambhir and Viru took as many singles as possible, the majority of runs came in boundaries. Opening the face of the bat and using the pace of the ball, which is considered near-blasphemy in Test cricket, is the easiest way to rotate the strike here, for there is hardly anyone manning the third-slip/fourth slip cordon. And once the powerplay overs are done, unless you are chasing a huge target, all you need to do is to rotate strike.

Even in this format, though, many players approached opening the batting differently. Kris Srikkanth started it and Mark Greatbatch took it to the next level, but it was Sanath Jayasuriya who changed the rules of the game. Jayasuriya, for me, was the Sehwag of ODI cricket. He took the aerial route right from the beginning and no one used the powerplays better than him. Gilchrist and Hayden also did something similar but Jayasuriya will always be remembered as the pioneer.

Opening in T20 cricket

Opening in the shortest format is all about aggression. There is no time to assess the pace and bounce, so you have to trust your instincts and take a bit of risk. In T20, it is as important to know your go-to areas as it is to know your off stump in Test cricket. An opener's endeavour is to find the fence at least twice an over. And if you don't manage to hit balls in your preferred areas, you must innovate or create the desired lengths and lines to find the fence. The first six overs can decide the future of a match in a T20 game and it is criminal to let them pass without inflicting enough damage. You can bide your time, but in this format that means a couple of deliveries at most.

If you are unbeaten at the end of the sixth over, it is your responsibility to bat deep into the innings. If one of the openers bats till the twelfth or thirteenth over, getting to a reasonable total is guaranteed. Having wickets in hand in the last seven overs gives everyone the licence to go berserk, and someone who has been there for such a long time might find accelerating a lot easier than a new guy walking in.

A lot has changed in cricket but perhaps nothing as drastically as opening the batting. Earlier, uncovered wickets, the quality of fast bowling and the pace at which the game was played dictated that openers be ultra-cautious. But today it is daredevilry that rules the roost.

CHASING 600

There are pitches that demand caution, for the captain winning the toss knows that there'll be swing and lateral movement for a session or two. And there are pitches that force the captain to bowl first, like the one we saw at Lord's for the second Test match between England and India in 2014. There was so much grass and moisture underneath that only a fool would decide otherwise. And then there are win-the-toss-bat-first pitches, mostly found in the subcontinent, that dictate batting first ten out of ten times, for there is not a strand of grass or moisture on the pitch. While batting first on such a track is an opportunity to cash in, it is not so easy to score on the same surface after the opposition has put up a score in excess of 600.

Big runs in the first innings give the batting team the advantage for a couple of reasons. One: to achieve that mammoth score you must bat for at least five sessions, which means the batsmen on the fielding side will be tired when it is their turn to bat. Second: the track, however flat it was at the start of the match, will deteriorate somewhat over those two days.

Let us try to get into the batsmen's minds while they wait for their turn to bat.

Once the opposition has won the toss and elected to bat, the batsmen in the fielding side switch off mentally. On flat tracks you don't think in terms of sessions but days; you'll seldom be required to bat after just a session or two.

Every now and then you tend to think about how you would have played on such a track and how unfortunate you are not to bat first. After that momentary indulgence in self-pity, you get back to the game and try to keep yourself entertained. You egg your teammates on and put some extra effort into making the day interesting and helping the team.

Then comes a time when the opposition is about seven or eight wickets down, having put up a huge score. One of my seniors, the late Raman (Lamba) bhaiyya, once told me that batsmen, especially openers, must stop chatting and cheering after the fall of the eighth wicket; they need to start thinking about their own batting, which might be a few balls away. Openers keep an eye on the opposition's dressing room, looking for a declaration. They also sometimes ask the tail-enders about their side's plans of declaring, if any. The problem is when the tail starts to wag and the opposition captain decides to prolong your agony. You can plan only so much mentally and keep yourself warm and loose for so long.

When the last wicket falls, or the declaration finally comes, the openers duly take the permission of the batsmen (it is against protocol to leave the ground before they do) and rush to the dressing room. After all, they get only ten minutes to get fresh, change into new clothes (at least a dry shirt) and put on their gear. It leaves very little time to gather your thoughts, and that is why most openers spend a couple of quiet minutes in their seats with their eyes closed just before walking on to the field.

Now, the scenes that greet the opening batsmen on the field are quite different from the ones they grew used to after nearly two days of play. There is a crowded slip cordon and most fielders are in attacking positions.

Once bowlers have a cushion of 600 runs, they become more effective, or at least more adventurous. They don't shy away from experimenting in order to dislodge the batsman and they don't worry about the runs conceded in the bargain.

Batsmen on the other hand are advised not to think in terms of runs—those scored by the opposition or how many they need to score themselves to get to safety. If you think about chasing a total of 650, it certainly sounds like a herculean task. Even if you think about 450 to avoid the follow-on, which is slightly less daunting, you are still starting off on the wrong foot. You can't be pessimistic right from the outset. A good idea would be to think about stitching together partnerships and batting sessions.

A huge first innings gives the opposition the leverage to try various things. They will invariably start with a conventional attack: two or three slips and perhaps a short leg. The bowling lines will be around off stump, the length on the fuller side. If that doesn't get the breakthrough, they will probably play with the patience of the batsmen by maintaining an outside-off-stump line with a heavily packed off-side field. I remember England trying the tactic against Michael Clarke in the 2005 Ashes. Eventually Clarke ended up dragging one back into his stumps, batting in his 90s.

If you think about chasing a total of 650, it certainly sounds like a herculean task. Even if you think about 450 to avoid the follow-on, which is slightly less daunting, you're still starting off on the wrong foot. You can't be pessimistic right from the outset.

If that doesn't work, sides opt for bowling into the batsman's ribs from around the wicket.

The spinners, too, maintain attacking lines and fields throughout. Even when the batsman is scoring freely, they will have a man at short-leg or silly point. That is exactly what India did during the last Test match, in Sydney, in 2004. Both Justin Langer and Matthew Hayden were well set, but I was kept at short-leg throughout.

The fielding team might also employ an inside-out field, which means having some fielders in catching positions and a few patrolling the fence.

The last resort would be to bowl into the rough. On other occasions, this particular option is used to restrict the batsmen from scoring runs, but when your team has a huge total on board you use it to attack.

A huge total ensures that the team batting second is never out of the woods and the team that put the total on board is never out of the game: a couple of quick wickets can change the game. Also, nine out of ten times, if the opposition has scored over 600 runs in the first innings of the Test match only two results are possible: a win for them or a draw.

In such situations, batting time is as important as scoring runs. Rahul Dravid once told me that saving a Test match is also an art. If your team manages to score enough to avoid the follow-on, you are generally safe. Otherwise, once again you start keeping an eye on the opposition's body language to assess if they will enforce the follow-on or not.

Regardless of whether they ask you to bat again or not, batting is not going to be easy whenever it comes next. The pressure increases manifold because there won't be another chance to make up for your mistake. Also, batting will rarely be easy on a fourth- or fifth-day pitch with a match to save.

While spinners are supposed to be the greatest threats on the last day, batting against the quick bowlers on a worn-out track with unpredictable bounce is equally difficult, especially in places like Australia where the cracks open up massively. Every now and then the ball hits a crack and behaves abnormally. That plays on the batsman's mind and can lead to errors of judgement.

When winning is not an option it is difficult to keep your spirits up for the remainder of a match. Batting in the fourth innings on the fifth day requires not only grit and determination but also a watertight technique. Not to mention that for batsmen the margin of error is remarkably small on the last day.

CONCENTRATION

Ever since I started playing cricket I have been told about the importance of concentration and how it is the key to batting for a long time and scoring a lot of runs. There has always been plenty of emphasis on this aspect of the game. I would often hear a commentator say that a lapse in concentration cost the batsman his wicket, or a coach telling me to concentrate harder whenever I couldn't put the bat to ball.

Though I understood the importance of concentration fairly early in my career, I didn't entirely understand the concept itself. And I wasn't the only one.

What exactly is concentration?

A few years ago I was selected to play in the Challenger Trophy (this was before I made my international debut). We had an interactive session with Geet Sethi, the billiards player, whose definition of concentration remains etched in my memory. He said that concentration is simply remaining in the present. The longer you can remain in the present, the greater your span of concentration. Sounds easy, right?

Over two decades of playing professional cricket has taught me that it isn't. The mind has the peculiar ability of wandering off at the first available moment, and it doesn't need any permission. You might be in the middle of an important match, playing an important knock or bowling the most crucial over, but the mind has a mind of its own. Two places it likes to wander off to are the past and the future.

It would either start feeling bad or good about what had happened in the past—the previous delivery, perhaps—and make you get disconnected from the present, or it would start worrying about or prematurely celebrating events in the future, getting away from the task at hand.

Whatever happened in the past or might happen in the future does not have, or at least should not have, any bearing on the ball you are going to bowl or play next. All that matters is what you do with that particular ball. Remaining in the present is the only way to concentrate.

One needs to start concentrating once the bowler starts his run-up and the concentration has to be at its peak from the time of delivery till the ball hits the bat. (Of course, this changes for fielders, who need to be alert till one of them fields the ball.)

How can you improve your concentration?

Most games of cricket go on for at least six hours at a time, with occasional breaks. For the layperson, concentrating for a few minutes at a time is quite difficult, let alone six hours. So the idea is to switch off after every delivery and then switch on before the next. Switching off means allowing the mind to wander away 'under supervision' for a few seconds before getting it back on track. This is not restricted to only batting and bowling; fielders do it too. One needs to relax before starting to concentrate again.

Batting or bowling in the nets can be instrumental in improving concentration, since one needs to concentrate ball after ball in that situation, with very little time in between (as there are usually about six or seven bowlers operating at all times).

The trigger movement

Most players follow a set routine—adjusting the equipment, or something else—that acts as a trigger to snap them out of wander mode and back to the game. Greg Chappell would look at the crowd after playing every ball; M.S. Dhoni fiddles with his bat and gloves; I scratch the leg-stump mark on the pitch with my shoe; Jason Gillespie used to stop for a few seconds and take a deep breath at the top of his run-up.

Staying in the game

While it is important to switch off and allow your mind to wander, one still needs to ensure that it doesn't drift too far away. For example, a captain has to still think about the field placements and plan his course of action, like bowling and fielding changes. A fielder is supposed to be always looking at the captain or bowler for instructions on any possible changes in the fielding position before starting to concentrate again. A batsman weighs his options of scoring runs off the next ball. I call this not-so-focused form of concentration 'staying in the game'.

The zone

Then there are some—we call them geniuses—who seemed to get into the zone at will: the state of mind where everything flows automatically. You don't consciously switch on or off, your mind doesn't wander into the past or the future, you are constantly aware of your surroundings and almost always play the ball on its merit or bowl where you want to bowl. We all have times when we get into such a state, but to do it on a consistent basis is an art that only a few have mastered. Sachin Tendulkar seemed to get into the zone more regularly than the rest.

How can one attain that state at will?

Honestly, I don't know for sure. I have gathered over the years that even the greatest minds can wander. Thoughts keep coming into your head regardless of whether you want them to. The best way to deal with them is to acknowledge their presence rather than trying to ignore them. Trying to push the thoughts away gets you more involved with the same thoughts and ends up taking you away from the task at hand. When you leave them unattended, they disappear. Tendulkar's innings in Sydney in 2004 is the perfect example of not paying heed to the thoughts that try to intrude. He didn't play a cover-drive for most, if not all, of his innings of over 200, and I refuse to believe that the thought of playing the shot didn't cross his mind, especially once he was set.

When are we most vulnerable to losing concentration?

I used to think that staying in the present was important only at the beginning of the innings. After all, it is only at the start, when we are plagued with self-doubt, that we are most susceptible to failure; once we get that elusive start, everything falls in place. But I have learned that I was mistaken. A loss of concentration can occur at any point during an innings, and most often does when you are feeling good, like after going past a milestone, when you drop your guard a bit.

I once asked Sunil Gavaskar about it and he said that when you reach a milestone, the mind takes you to the ones you love most. You feel an immediate connection to those close to you who are watching you achieve the feat and your heart goes out to them, and with it, takes your mind too. You thank everyone on the ground by raising the bat, thank God for his blessings and your family members in your heart. At such times the mind is anywhere but on the cricket field and you often end up taking the long walk back before realizing what has happened. Sunny bhai's advice to me was to recognize that emotional surge and allow yourself a little time to regroup; perhaps spending a few overs at the non-striker's end at such times is a good idea.

The external factors

Bowlers and fielders, especially the ones close to the bat, often try to talk the batsman into playing a poor stroke. A few batsmen succumb to the tactic and lose focus; the majority have their own ways of dealing with it.

Sunny bhai also told me that the best way is to ignore the comments and even avoid eye contact with the talkers. On the contrary, someone like Matthew Hayden relishes a chat with the bowler and the fielders. Then there is Brian Lara. The

Indian team would decide before the start of a series against West Indies to leave him alone, because if you try to get under his skin he starts concentrating harder and then is almost impossible to dislodge.

Even the crowd has a role to play. But contrary to popular belief, a hostile crowd doesn't have as much of an impact as a cheering crowd.

I remember getting hit on the helmet in Melbourne during the Boxing Day Test in 2003, and 70,000 people cheered Brett Lee and Co. to do it again. But the only effect it had on my game plan was to make me more determined. On the other hand only 30,000 people egging me on to hit another four off Daniel Vettori in my debut Test, in Ahmedabad, was enough to lure me into a false stroke. I got ahead of myself and was dismissed.

We now know that regardless of whether we know the definition of concentration or not, whether we play cricket—or any other sport for that matter—remaining in the present is the essence to being successful. We all do it unconsciously, and perhaps that is why we slip out of it without knowing, but if we manage to do it consciously, at will, keeping close tabs on our mind, we will be able to control it better and produce better results.

DEATH BOWLING AND BATTING

The bowler came sprinting in his run-up and unleashed his trademark lethal reverse swinging toe-crushers. But the man on the batting end had thought it through; he managed to get under the deliveries and hit them out of the park.

This is a segment from the epic India–Pakistan encounter in the 1996 World Cup quarter-final in Bangalore. The bowler was Waqar Younis and the batsman, Ajay Jadeja. It was perhaps my first introduction to the potential of the death overs and their effect on the upshot of a thrilling contest.

Death overs are an unabashed display of the intent to win come what may. It is not a time when cricketers play hide-and-seek. Both bowler and batsman know each other's intentions as well as they know their own. A bowler is looking to minimize the damage and the batsman is sure to throw caution to the wind. For the players involved, it is their chance to get their team home. These are the glory boys but also the ones who are made villains if the ball misses the target by an inch—either on the bat, eluding the sweet spot, or turning from an intended yorker into a full toss or a half-volley.

Bowling

While there are three common lengths bowlers use towards the end—yorkers, bouncers and back of length effort ball that hits high on the bat, the best bet is to bowl a yorker and hope to err on the side of being full, because low full-tosses are tougher to hit than half-volleys.

Of late, though, batsmen have begun to open their shoulders and go deep inside the crease to get under these yorkers. The so-called toe-crushers no longer bother batsmen like Kieron Pollard and M.S. Dhoni, who send them sailing over long on and midwicket.

For the bowler, the length is sacrosanct when bowling to such batsmen, and the line favours the off: bowling yorkers outside off stump is often an effective way of controlling the damage; but you need to strengthen the field square on the off side for it to work. I have seen Shane Warne post three fielders in the deep, in the area between point and third man, while bringing fine leg, midwicket and even mid-on, inside the circle. It will take special skills to drag a full ball from outside off towards fine leg.

The only length ball a bowler can bowl is one with no pace on it, for balls of normal pace are guaranteed to be dismissed.

The length of a slower delivery ought to change with the surface too. On surfaces with good bounce it is important to not pitch it too short, for it will sit up to get hit. The field placement is also crucial for the success of a slower delivery. Since it doesn't have the pace to go past the third-man fielder, it is only wise to bring him inside the circle. On the other hand, having the midwicket fielder on the fence is almost mandatory.

The bouncer, if executed properly, is one of the most

difficult balls to get away in the death overs. There are a few variations of the delivery but their use depends on the pitch. The slower bouncer isn't that handy on slow surfaces where the ball keeps low, because it rarely reaches the optimum height to cause discomfort. A good quick bouncer is the way to go in the subcontinent, while bowling slower bouncers isn't a bad option on hard and bouncy tracks. The correct field placement enhances the chances of the bouncer's effectiveness. You need fine leg, square leg, and even third man (in case of an upper cut) back on the fence, but you can always bring mid-off inside the circle.

These changes in the field must come from the bowler, for he is the one who knows what he is going to deliver next. John Buchanan tried a system of signals with Kolkata Knight Riders in the second season of the IPL, with the bowler indicating what his intended next ball would be. It didn't work as it should have because it wasn't the bowler but the fielding captain who took the call on what fields to have; but implemented properly it can work wonders, especially in the slog overs.

Batting

Batting in the final overs is as specialized a job as opening the innings. Not only do you need special skill sets, at times you need brute strength to clear the fence.

While you identify your strengths as a batsman and must go for broke if you get a ball in your area, it is highly unlikely that you will, without doing something out of the box. For example, if you like going over midwicket, be assured that most balls to you will finish outside off, since good bowlers work to a plan. To make things work in your favour you must out-think the bowler and create the desired line and length yourself. It is something Sachin Tendulkar did with aplomb during his double-century against the South Africans in Gwalior. He constantly moved about in the crease to keep the bowler guessing.

Since as a batsman you are also aware of the bowler's three desired lengths, you can take a calculated risk, guessing what the next ball will be, leaving the option of taking a single as your last resort.

While being a little cheeky doesn't hurt, the better players at the end of an innings are the ones who maintain a solid base all the time. You rarely saw people like Lance Klusener hit a shot while off position or off balance, because it is almost impossible to get the power or timing if the base and the head are not stable.

Another point a batsman needs to keep in mind is to not get too close to the ball, for you need room to swing the arms; also, staying away from the ball a little is mandatory to help you get under it for elevation. Both Dhoni and Suresh Raina are brilliant when it comes to clearing the front leg out of the way to create room, going slightly deeper in the crease to get under the full ball and also staying away to allow the arms to swing free for the off-target length ball. Then there is A.B. de Villiers who has invented a new way of countering death bowling—he moves around, goes down on one knee and then sweeps or reverse sweeps and intended yorker. But he belongs to the category of genuines.

It is also wise to keep a close eye on the constantly changing field positions, so you have an insight into the bowler's thinking and can then prepare yourself accordingly.

While chasing a target, it is imperative to think in terms of balls, not overs. Keeping a calm head while calculating your chances is what separates a good finisher from an average middle-order player. If you need 36 off 24 balls, it takes only four hits to the fence to bring the rather daunting-looking equation down to a more realistic run-a-ball. But thinking of getting nine an over can create panic.

Batting in the death overs may not be the most pleasing sight for a purist, but if observed closely, the smaller battles within the big one make for interesting viewing. How a batsman reads the bowler's mind, or vice versa, speaks volumes about the strength of a player's character. Imagine the pressure a bowler must feel while bowling the last over, or the last ball of the match, with the opposition needing only a boundary for victory.

Things were not so tough for bowlers when the same ball was used till the fiftieth over, because the reverse swing allowed bowlers to have more than a say in proceedings. You would rarely see Wasim Akram shy away from these demanding situations. On the contrary, his skill in making the old ball talk allowed him to dictate terms. But since two new balls are used—one from each end—these days, the bowler's job is cut out for him.

Make no mistake though, the man who is expected to hit the last ball to the fence is under tremendous pressure too. It is the one who holds his nerve in the end who survives. Maybe that is why the term 'death overs' was coined, for failure isn't an option at that stage.

DECODING THE FIRST ODI DOUBLE TON

'I looked to put pressure on the bowlers right from the start of the match,' Sachin Tendulkar wrote in his reply to my text message to him after his epic 200. Reading his text made me wonder. I have never got close to scoring a double-century in a limited-overs match. Not even against club sides in England. I have scored a few centuries in List A matches and a few doubles in first-class cricket, but to be honest, even the thought of scoring a double-century in limited-overs cricket has never crossed my mind.

What is so arduous about a double-century that only six men in the history of the game can boast of having achieved the milestone?

There are quite a few prerequisites that anyone who wants to even come close to what so few batsmen have achieved must meet. Since you need to bat the entire fifty overs, or near enough, it is almost mandatory that you either open or bat one-down. Some may argue that even the No. 4 has a chance if the team loses two wickets in the first two overs. But to score a double-century you have to be aggressive right from the outset and if you walk in after the team has lost two early wickets, chances are you will be restrained. You will be required to rein in your natural attacking instincts to play percentage cricket, at least for a little while, and so you will lose out on precious time. If you are to get anywhere close to scoring a double, time is at a premium.

When Tendulkar said he looked to put pressure on bowlers, he perhaps meant that you must start hitting the ball really well from the beginning. It is equivalent to hitting the first ball for four and keeping that up for the rest of the innings. We have seen Virender Sehwag or Adam Gilchrist hit a boundary off the first ball many times. Even I have done it a few times in my career. But that, of course, has never translated into a double-century. So what it means here is that the batsman sees the ball well and his hands and feet move in sync from the moment he walks in.

'My state of mind was the same throughout the innings,' Tendulkar said. I think he meant he got into the zone early. The zone is like a state of nirvana: a certain stillness within, when everything flows naturally and things around you don't interrupt your inner harmony. You move at your own pace. The results are a by-product of that. Most players manage to reach this state from time to time but it rarely lasts for the entire duration of an innings. Some achieve it for a few minutes, others for an hour or so. Then you lose concentration and are lured into doing silly things—sometimes by your own over-confidence, sometimes by the bowling.

When a batsman is in top form, he rarely bats against

the opposition. Instead he competes with himself to prevent turning over-confident. He must forget he is in great touch and start from scratch every single time. During the course of the innings he needs to remind himself not to go overboard. Most people don't achieve this level of self-realization while batting really well.

The lack of effort required to score runs leads to boredom. When the opposition can't challenge you, you stretch yourself. You try to play a reverse-sweep or a switch-hit. And if you pull it off, you try the same against a fast bowler and usually lose your wicket. We have seen Sehwag doing so on a number of occasions. But Tendulkar managed to stay in the zone all the way through and didn't try to outplay himself, which is a very difficult thing to do. Perhaps that explains why only five players got to the landmark for so long.

I think batting first is also an advantage when playing such innings because you are not distracted by a target, an asking rate or pressure. The thought of playing a few dot balls doesn't play on your mind as heavily as it would while chasing a huge target. Also, to score a double-century while chasing, the target must be in excess of 350 runs. That means you are chasing seven runs an over and that cannot be achieved alone. Neither you nor your partner can afford to play dot balls. If he does, you have to try and make up by playing more aggressively than you already are.

'Whatever shots I planned worked for me that day,' Tendulkar said modestly. What actually happened was, he lured fast bowlers into bowling full by going deep inside the crease and they obliged. Knowing that the bowlers would target the stumps, he walked across, exposing his leg stump, and dispatched them to the square-leg boundary. Tendulkar made them bowl exactly where he wanted them to.

I remember Matthew Hayden would do something similar. He would walk down the track to fast bowlers, needling them into bowling bouncers. The bowlers who fell for it were dispatched with ease. But this kind of approach is an art only a few have mastered.

'I wasn't tired at the end. I could have gone on for more overs comfortably,' Tendulkar wrote at the end of the text. Batting anything over thirty overs in an ODI is physically challenging. That Tendulkar still had gas in the tank for more tells us how fit he is physically and mentally.

What was most impressive about his innings was not the milestone but how he got there. Some would think a certain amount of slogging is almost mandatory to score a double, but Tendulkar proved that wrong. He started with flowing cover drives and deft touches off his pads and continued to bat that way till the end. He did improvise along the way but didn't play a scoop or a switch-hit because he didn't need to. Getting the front leg out of the way to clear the off side, walking across the stumps to hit balls outside off to leg or using the crease were enough. That indicates the freedom his impeccable technique gives him.

A lot of aggressive players have opened, batted first, dominated the bowling and been physically fit. But all of it hasn't been and will not be enough to score double-centuries in fifty-overs cricket. Yet it won't be like the four-minute-mile barrier, which was broken many times. It needed a Tendulkar to break this particular barrier and it will need an equally gifted and special player to do it again.

Special note: Four batsmen have managed to score an ODI double century since Tendulkar's feat and all of them have ticked the boxes mentioned in this essay—all were openers and their team batted first.

FEVER PITCH

The term 'catch 22' could very well have been coined for the twenty-two yards of the cricket pitch. You can never truly decipher its code completely. Perhaps the greatest catch in cricket is sussing a pitch out, fine-tuning play and thus finding your feet.

Ever wondered how batsmen read a pitch and decide what kind of game will be best suited to it? Or how bowlers decide how to operate on different surfaces? While reading a wicket is an art that only a few have mastered, players who know their game well tend to smarten up their play to exploit the pitch. The endeavour is always to give yourself the best chance to succeed under the circumstances. While changing your game overnight isn't possible, you try to curb certain instincts and modify your game to succeed. Apart from the track, one also needs to deal with the opposition, but there is only so much you can do with that. You can identify threats and opportunities, but it is the track that demands a bigger adjustment.

Bouncy wickets

Once you know as a batsman that the track has more bounce

than most others—like at, say, Perth—you set your game plan accordingly.

Strokes off the back foot are considered to be the best bet, but you need to be precise with your shot selection while playing them. On a track with extra bounce, the drive off the back foot isn't exactly a paying shot, unless you pick the right length and line. On such tracks it is rather difficult to get on top of the bounce—which you need to do to play an effective back-foot drive—and hence the chances of nicking it to the keeper are pretty high.

Playing a square-cut is a safer option, but once again, only if you execute it well. Keeping the square-cut down is a challenge on such surfaces and you shouldn't shy away from taking the aerial route. Remember Sachin Tendulkar playing all those shots over the slip cordon in Perth?

Another thing to keep in mind is that all edges will easily carry to the slips and the wicketkeeper, so you need to be extra careful when you play shots around the off stump. At the same time, you can trust the bounce while leaving the ball. The ideal game plan on such surfaces is to score most of your runs on the back foot, wait for a half-volley to score off the front foot and avoid playing defensive strokes to balls that can be left alone. On the subject of leaving the ball alone, mostly it is about picking the line correctly, for if you leave the ball that is too close to you, you would be a sitting duck. But on pitches with more bounce you can trust the bounce and leave the ball on length even if you misread the line. I did that quite a bit during the tour to Australia in 2003-04.

As a bowler you try not to get carried away with the bounce and bowl slightly fuller than you otherwise would. The endeavour should be to bring the batsman forward as much as possible.

Wickets with sideways movement

Batsmen don't really look forward to tracks that offer a lot of sideways movement—like Headingley or Brisbane—because you need to have watertight technique and a lot of discipline to succeed on them. Surviving on these pitches also requires a lot of guesswork, patience and clarity in terms of game plan.

For starters, you can be sure bowlers will bowl full and so you must prepare yourself to play a lot of deliveries on the front foot. You also need a sound knowledge of where your off stump is, because you will be required to leave a lot of deliveries alone. Most players draw an imaginary line outside the off stump, which works as an indicator: anything pitched outside that line is to be left alone.

Playing in the second line, close to the body and as late as possible, are a few points you need to remember through your innings. All of this could bog you down, and that is why it is imperative to have a positive mindset. It not only helps you score runs off loose balls, it doesn't allow the bowler to work on a plan.

For bowlers, it is important to pitch the ball fuller to add swing to the already existing seam movement, but avoid getting carried away and bowling half-volleys. If lateral movement off the pitch is on offer, you must allow that to take place by keeping the length slightly short but not short enough that can be negotiated off the back-foot. Like the batsman, the bowler needs to be equally patient in sticking to the right lines if he doesn't get edges right away. There is always the temptation to try swinging the ball from leg stump, which often results in a boundary. The mantra to success is to be persistent with a probing line.

Dust bowls

Playing on dust bowls is as challenging as playing on seaming tracks, for there is enough sideways movement available off the surface to trouble the batsman. You need to be decisive with your foot movement, to either get to the pitch of the ball or go deep inside the crease to get on top of the spin. Indecisiveness will almost definitely get you into trouble.

Another important trait needed to succeed on rank turners is to remain positive and take calculated risks. Attacking field positions combined with vicious turn doesn't allow you to manoeuvre the ball for singles, so punishing the occasional loose balls and going over the top are imperative. Playing against the spin is a no-no unless you are V.V.S. Laxman.

As a batsman, you know that scoring runs off spinners won't be easy, so you try to score as many as possible against the quick bowlers.

As for the fast bowlers, they know that most batsmen will be dismissed in front of the stumps, and that is why they resort to taking the pace off the ball and bowling cutters instead of swing. Spinners, on the other hand, thrive in these conditions; but they also need to be patient and not get ahead of themselves. They need to bowl a little quicker in the air while imparting more rotations on the ball. This not only gives less time to the batsman to adjust but also gives the bowler more off the surface.

Unusual tracks

Then there are certain wickets that need special attention, like the one at Lord's. That particular track has a slope and you need to be extra careful to succeed. You must take the slope

> On a dodgy wicket in a first-class match once, Sehwag kept walking down the track and swinging wildly. He was intentionally missing the ball. His plan was to force the bowler to bowl the next ball shorter, and it worked.

into account while playing because the ball deviates off the surface both ways, depending on which way the slope is. The same goes for the bowlers, for their straight-down-the-track delivery often ends up either on leg stump or slightly outside off.

The ideal batting surface

The ideal pitch for batsmen would have true bounce and very little sideways movement. While it is extremely easy to bat on such surfaces and they require very little imagination or planning, you still need to keep a few things in mind. To begin with, you must keep reminding yourself to not get carried away. Since batting seems so easy, there is always the temptation to up the ante by pulling off adventurous shots, which often lead to your downfall. Playing percentage cricket and negotiating each ball on its merit is enough to seal the deal.

While such surfaces are paradise for batsmen, they are a nightmare for bowlers. All they can do is try and avoid doing anything that would add to their agony i.e. stick to the basics and maintain a good line and length. Yes, they need to use variety to fox the batsman, but it is imperative to have patience and keep these variations to a minimum—every boundary conceded will deflate the bowler and give the batsman more confidence.

Every player draws up a mental list of do's and don'ts for different surfaces. Even Virender Sehwag, whose only game plan seems to be to see and hit the ball, has a plan every time he goes out to bat. On a dodgy wicket in a first-class match once, he kept walking down the track and swinging wildly. I was at the other end and tried to reason with him. You would be surprised to learn that he was intentionally missing the ball. His plan was to force the bowler to bowl the next ball shorter, and it worked. On docile tracks, Zaheer Khan bowled at only about 65–70 per cent capacity in the afternoon session of a Test match, for he knew that the only chance of taking wickets on such surfaces was when the ball is new or when it started reversing. Rahul Dravid and Sanjay Bangar executed a perfect plan at Headingley in 2002, which set up that historic Indian victory. There are plenty of such examples.

While a competitive team always looks the most potent threat, it is the wicket that can supersede all game plans. It wouldn't be an exaggeration to call the pitch the twelfth man.

FIELDING AT SHORT-LEG

What does the close-in fielder focus on?

While standing at short-leg or silly point, I focus on the body language of the batsman, his foot movements and his back-lift. These three aspects give away the length of the ball and the kind of shot the batsman is looking to play.

Most catches come when the batsman is playing a defensive shot and the likelihood of those is a lot higher if he is on the front foot. The back-lift is a lot shorter if the batsman is playing a defensive shot except if it is a batsman who always opts for a high back-lift. For example, fielding to someone like Yuvraj Singh or Virender Sehwag is extremely difficult because their high back-lift doesn't give away anything: every time they lift the bat you think they are preparing for an aggressive shot, but it could just as well end up being a defensive prod.

Personally I don't like to look at the bowler to gauge the length of the ball because it involves moving my neck, which in turn means shifting focus to the batsman once the ball is released. It is not only taxing but could also hamper your concentration on the subject, the batsman.

The right posture

A lot of players go into a full squat while fielding at short leg, but I prefer a half squat. The disadvantage of going down fully is that the moment the batsman plays the shot, your first reaction is to get up. Your eye level changes the moment you get up, which makes you lose focus. But if you are in a half squat, there is no need to get up. Such a posture is slightly more crouched than the one used while standing in the slips.

The key is to stay low, with the hands close to the ground, which means that the back is perpetually bent. This is very taxing, both on the lower back and thighs.

Not being too tall is also an advantage. It makes staying low easier and the lower centre of gravity allows the shorter person to be more agile compared to taller men. No wonder most good close-in fielders aren't the tallest men around.

Evasive action

A key difference between fielding at short leg and silly point is the way the fielder protects himself when the ball is hit. At short leg you must go down as much as possible and become as small as you can: batsmen rarely try to keep the ball down while pulling or sweeping.

At silly point the fielder must jump to defend, because batsmen rarely try to hit the ball in the air on the off side. They aim to keep the ball along the ground, and hence you can avoid the line of the ball by jumping. While jumping you must remember not to turn your back towards the batsman because all your protective gear (shin-pads, abdominal guard and helmet) are worn on the front. Keeping an eye on the ball helps too!

Why is it that only batsmen are close-in fielders?

We see only pure batsmen taking up these positions. One of the reasons is the need batsmen feel to contribute in the team's success by fielding and cheering. Not that the bowlers are not required to field and cheer, but I personally think that it is the duty of batsmen to lead the pack in these aspects. A batsman's contribution is a bit of a gamble: even the best succeed only about six out of ten times, and we lesser mortals, even fewer. Practically, as a batsman you simply can't contribute in every game, and that is where fielding and cheering comes in.

The second reason is to do with temperament. Standing close to the bat requires a certain amount of concentration, and it can also be quite demanding on the legs.

Yet another reason is that fielding in catching positions can hurt your fingers, and bowlers' fingers and arms are far more precious than those of batsmen.

Also, the bowlers need to conserve their brains and energy to plan their wickets, rather than waste them on the chatting that is part of the job when you field close to the bat: you need to constantly remind the batsman of your presence.

Why only young batsmen or newcomers?

Close-in fielding positions are considered dangerous and physically demanding, and that is why—though no one likes to admit it—the job is assigned to the juniors. It is a system I have been part of, and I don't have any complaints about it. I used to be a regular in these positions for a few years after my first-class debut. But when I graduated to senior level, I started fielding in slip cordon, a position I was pretty good at right from the start but never got the opportunity to field in, in international cricket.

It is something that happened with Rahul Dravid as well. He is one of the finest fielders at short leg, but when new guys like me came into the side, he let us take over. Moreover, I felt like it was my duty to give him a break.

The only problem I faced from time to time was that as an opener I got only ten minutes between innings, and it takes much longer than that to get rid of the tiredness of fielding up close. I would always try to talk someone else into fielding at short leg once the opposition had lost eight wickets, but unfortunately it didn't work every time.

Side effects

At times, batsmen take the chat from the close-in fielders personally. I remember New Zealand's Lou Vincent, fed up of my chirping, told me to either shut up or face the consequences. I didn't stop and the next ball, from Anil Kumble, was hit directly into my knees. It was a short-pitched delivery and Lou was batting on 100; so instead of hitting it to the fence he chose to target me. It hit my knee, which had been operated on a while ago, and caused quite some pain, but I couldn't show it. It was a little mean of him to react that way, but that is how the game is played at the highest level. He got out to the next delivery and I celebrated as if it was my first Test wicket.

The importance of the bowler

Your confidence while fielding at short leg or silly point depends on the quality of the bowler and the way a particular batsman plays. I would feel extremely confident when Anil bowled, because he rarely bowled a short ball that could be pulled; he is also a tough bowler to sweep. But when a part-time bowler was on, I would be praying incessantly.

I remember fielding at short leg for Ambati Rayudu on an A tour. He would bowl a full toss or a half-tracker between good-length deliveries. Abhijit Kale had already been hit on the head off Rayudu's bowling, and I was naturally wary. The moment he pitched short—and these were the only times I would turn to watch his release—I would lie flat, face down, on the ground. Everyone laughed, but the balls were so short that squatting there would have made me a sitting duck.

Is it scary?

The correct answer would be a firm 'no', but the honest answer is 'yes'. I have been scared a few times. For example, while fielding at short leg when Matthew Hayden and Justin Langer were sweeping almost everything. The shots were so ferocious that the fielders at long leg—and this was at huge grounds like the MCG and SCG—were ducking for cover. A few yards left or right of them meant a boundary.

I got a real fright once when the ball hit my helmet on its way to crashing into the fence, bouncing only once in between.

I truly enjoyed my stint at short leg, but it would be inhuman to not be scared—and that has nothing to do with being cowardly. Besides, I did not fear the pain a blow might inflict; I feared something scarier: getting hit on the arm or fingers, which might jeopardise my batting in the next innings, next Test, or perhaps the rest of my career.

I have been hit many times and I don't fear the pain. I have dropped my wrists on a number of occasions on purpose and allowed the ball to hit me in the chest or on the shoulder. I have also made the odd error of judgement by ducking when the ball wasn't all that short or didn't bounce as expected, and hence have had the ball smash into my body.

I recognize the pain a cricket ball can cause, and trust me, it isn't threatening. The key is knowing where the ball is going to hit you and at what speed. The moment I decide to allow the ball to hit me, the brain processes that information and prepares the body. It might sound weird, but once you know it is going to hit you, it doesn't hurt all that much.

Expecting the ball

What has always worked for me is that, regardless of where I'm fielding, I expect the ball to come to me. While standing at short leg or silly point, I would try to put my hand to every ball that went past me, barring the full-fledged pull, sweep or cover-drive. Whether I managed to get a finger to it, block it, catch or miss it was inconsequential. Perhaps that is why I managed to hold on to a few good catches.

Also, you need to sharpen your reflexes because they are your only allies when it comes to taking a catch or defending yourself.

Placing yourself

The angle at which you field is based on the way a particular batsman bats and how much the ball is turning off the surface. Even the distance from the bat is dictated by the speed of the ball, bounce in the pitch, the kind of shots a batsman plays, and nowadays the quality of the pads.

The fielder needs to be a lot closer to the bat for people like Dravid, who offer a dead bat, compared to those who jab at the ball, like Darren Sammy does every time. Fielders need to be further away from the bat if the batsman is using stronger leg-guards, like Sachin Tendulkar and some New Zealand batsmen. You also stand a bit further away when a quick bowler is bowling.

Protection

I can't dream of going close to the batsman without wearing enough protection, so it is tough to even imagine how the late Eknath Solkar did it—and with distinction at that. Life has become a lot better with helmets, shin-pads and other protective gear. It helps to know that you won't die if the ball hits you on the head—though not enough to make you completely carefree.

While one can wear chest-pads, shin-pads, helmets and so on, there are still enough areas left exposed where a strike could prove fatal. I can never forget the untimely demise of Raman Lamba, who was my senior and a mentor of sorts to me. Of course, he wasn't wearing even a helmet, but we have all stood many a time for a ball or two without wearing any protection.

I remember borrowing a chest-guard from Dravid and using it to protect my ribs in Sydney. After a few sweep shots missed me by a whisker, Sachin asked me which side I was wearing the chest pad on. I wore it on the right, but without realizing it, I kept moving towards my right, thereby exposing my unprotected left side. Sachin pointed this out and I corrected it immediately.

FIELDING POSITIONS

Cricket, despite being a team sport, is strictly an individual event until the batsman hits the ball. The bowler initiates the action and only after the batsman reacts are others spurred into action. But the collective effort of the remaining ten players on the field, at times, makes or breaks the game. That is why teams looking to make a mark focus a lot on fielding to make up for their lack of skill and experience with bat and ball. Sri Lanka, Bangladesh and Zimbabwe did so in their early stages.

The same goes for teams gunning for the top perch. Since the difference in skills isn't much at that level, they try to get an edge over the opposition with their fielding. Australia and South Africa often steal a march over the others in this department.

While cricketers are becoming multi-dimensional, there is still enough room for specialists in all three departments. Like batting and bowling, there are a lot of positions in the field that need to be manned by fielders with special skills. At point and square leg you need agility to intercept a ball rapidly spinning away from you, and in slips you need a bagful of concentration and quick reflexes. You ought to be brilliant at covering ground and must have a rocket throw to be an effective fielder on the fence.

Slips

Standing at slip is as specialized a position as opening the batting. It requires concentration, patience, quick reflexes and good hands. It can be as tiring as batting for six hours because you must expect every ball to come your way but may not get even one the entire day. That is why switching on and off between deliveries is extremely important. Good fielders—Mohammad Azharuddin was one—wait till the very last moment to switch on, which is only after the bowler jumps in his delivery stride.

Every slip fielder, depending on where he stands, needs to look out for certain things. For example, the first slip must follow the path of the ball right from the moment it leaves the bowler's hand. Those from second slip to gully are advised to concentrate on the outer edge of the bat. Keeping the head still is paramount while fielding in the slip cordon. While you can watch the bowler and follow the path of the ball to the batsman without moving your head from first slip, it is almost impossible to do so while standing wider.

While it is important to field with soft hands to avoid the ball popping out, on the basis of my experience and from watching others, it is equally important to keep your hands firm to counter the pace at which the ball is travelling.

Staying low—maintaining a low centre of gravity—and keeping your weight on the inside of the balls of your feet are also important. That not only helps you to take low catches but also allows for swift sideways movement. Mark Taylor used to stand at slip with his knees bent inwards to shift the weight to the inside of the balls of his feet.

Remember to open your toes in the direction of the ball. It will allow you to follow the ball better and also increases your reach. Mark Waugh took those catches that seemed to have gone past him with brilliant reflexes, great hands and by opening his toes.

Gully

Perhaps the toughest place to field. Most catches that go to gully are hit very hard and you need super-quick reflexes to catch them. In ODIs, the fielder at gully is only 15 metres away, which, under normal circumstances gives you very little time to react, let alone try to catch a Virender Sehwag cut off Shoaib Akhtar. That is why in ODIs most teams prefer to keep two slips instead of a slip and a gully.

Standing at gully to spinners is tougher. The only way of taking a catch off a spinner is when the batsman has played a front-foot shot: you get more time to react and the ball is relatively slower. The moment a batsman goes on the back foot and plays an aggressive shot, you pray it doesn't come your way because your reflexes might not be sharp enough to save you. The best fielder I have seen at gully is Delhi's Ranji player K.P. Bhaskar. Basics of fielding at gully are identical to fielding at second and third slip, for the focus is always on the edge of the bat and staying low is paramount.

Point and square leg

This is also a specialist position, usually manned by the quickest fielders in the team. At point, the ball spins rapidly away from you, so you need to be alert to intercept, recover the ball and return accurately. This is where getting a good start and cutting angles come in. Jonty Rhodes, arguably the best fielder at point, used to take a longish start and then hop into a near-stationary position just before the ball was hit. The stationary position is called 'base-up' and it is extremely important to attain at the time the batsman hits the ball because it is not possible to move sideways when the body is in forward motion. By taking a longish start, Rhodes would also reduce the angles. The closer you are to the batsman, the smaller the angles; the farther you are, the greater the angle and hence that much tougher to stop. You will need good reflexes if you come too close because the ball is moving faster, but good fielders back their reflexes to do the job.

While playing for the Kolkata Knight Riders, Ricky Ponting told us the importance of getting in line with the target while throwing. To hit the stumps consistently, you must get into the right position as soon as possible. Perhaps that is the reason Ponting hits the stumps more than the rest. At times, you may have to throw while off balance, but it should be an aberration and not a norm.

Fielding in the covers and at midwicket also requires similar skills. But fielders at those positions don't have to deal with the ball spinning away from them.

The deep

If fielding in the thirty-yard circle is mostly about intercepting, fielding at the fence is about getting in the right position to receive the ball. The boundary runners cover the ground quicker than the rest and possess good throwing arms. They must also cut angles instead of running in an arc. This saves time and gets them closer to the target.

Boundary fielders are usually good catchers of the long ball too. If you have the time to get under the ball and stabilise yourself before catching, you have more chances to succeed.

Focus

Though you get watchful the moment the ball is hit in your direction, it is impossible to train your concentration on it all the way through. There are way too many things in the frame—the batsman, the ground, other fielders, the crowd, etc. So initially you just focus on getting into the right position while keeping an eye on the ball. This is called *soft focus*.

But when the ball is only a few yards away, everything else fades away into oblivion and you start focusing completely on the ball, all the way into your hands. This is *hard focus*.

Sliding and diving

Sliding and stopping the ball is an effective way to prevent runs and also, if managed right, to get up and into the right position to throw quickly. The trick is to time your slide in such a way that you go past the ball. You can pull out of a slide whenever you want, but it is not possible to extend a slide beyond a point.

While diving to catch, it is important you avoid your elbows hitting the ground, for that can make the ball pop out on landing. Good core strength allows you to recover quickly after diving.

A good fielding unit can make an ordinary bowling line-up

effective and a poor fielding performance can make a good bowling line-up look ordinary. Unlike batting and bowling, fielding has little to do with luck. Pitches or your opponents' skills don't matter. You won't get a great ball, as you might while batting, or a belter of a track as while bowling. The conditions mostly remain the same throughout the match and for both teams.

When Azhar led the Indian team to South Africa in 1992-93, after a couple of games they decided to either not play the square cut at all or to run only after the ball had passed the wall called Rhodes. On bouncy tracks, the square cut is your bread-and-butter shot, and the area behind point is the most productive region in which to score runs. Imagine a team eliminating it from their game plan because of one fielder. And if one fielder could do that, imagine the impact a good fielding unit can have on the opposition.

FINDING FORM

'The moment I'm hitting the on-drive correctly, I know I'm in form,' Rahul Dravid once said. Gautam Gambhir too thought much the same: 'When my head is not falling over, I know I'm in form.' The catchphrase here is 'in form'. Almost every cricketer talks of this holy word, and when going through a bad patch he will give an arm to get it back. But like with most things, you value form only when you are out of it.

What exactly is being 'in form'?

The dictionary explains 'form' in different ways, but for cricketers it is a state of uncluttered mind: when everything falls in place and you don't have to worry about where the next run or the next wicket will come from. When in form, it happens by itself. When in form, your focus is on the next ball, not on the one that just went past your bat. You find gaps when in form, fielders when out of it.

Like Dravid and Gambhir, all cricketers know when they are in form. But while you can usually gauge it by how you do the things you find most difficult to do, there is more to it than just realizing your head is not falling over anymore. It takes a combination of things to happen simultaneously.

For batsmen it starts with watching the ball early, judging the length and line to perfection, and then moving their feet swiftly to get their body in position to deal with the ball. For bowlers it starts with the run-up, getting the jump and balance right and then the perfect wrist position for release. The desired shot or delivery is merely the outcome of having everything else in order.

Can form be achieved?

There isn't a set formula but constant efforts will take you there eventually. Different players approach their bad patches differently. While most prefer to hit the nets and practise as much as possible, some opt to stay away from the game for a while. I belong to the camp that practises for hours. Ricky Ponting is a part of the other one. While he believes in both quality and quantity of practice, when not in form he likes to go into the match slightly under-prepared, especially when he is hitting the ball well in the nets. He believes good batting in the nets, at times, gives you false confidence. So instead of working your way out of the slump, you fall prey to the temptation of hitting the big shots you would in the nets.

Greg Chappell has another way of dealing with poor form. He says: 'When not in form you should look back at your career stats. More often than not you'd find that you scored runs in every fourth or fifth innings, and hence every innings of low score is actually taking you closer to the innings in which you would score runs.' I think it is a great way to deal with the disappointment of getting out cheaply and handle the bad times.

As kids, we were told to remember good innings from the past from which to draw confidence. Virender Sehwag does that by watching videos of his innings. That is the best way to find the faults and work towards rectifying them.

> When in form, your focus is on the next ball, not on the one that just went past your bat. You find gaps when in form, fielders when out of it.

You could also try spending more time in the middle. Some batsmen like to hit their way out of a bad patch. I prefer fighting it out. During a bad patch in the 2006-07 Duleep Trophy I somehow managed to spend an hour on the crease against East Zone. I didn't get many runs in the game but struck gold in the final against Sri Lanka A. I couldn't put a finger on what changed my fortune except for the time spent on the crease in the previous game.

In form does not equal autopilot

So once in form, you expect things to be pretty smooth. Not quite. Even Sangakarra, who was in sublime form during the 2015 World Cup, didn't have it easy. Now his challenge is to keep this form going for as long as possible. There will be a temptation to do something extraordinary or outrageous since he seems to be scoring runs at will. He will need to keep that temptation at bay and continue doing the basics right.

A bad patch is inevitable so batsmen try to score enough while in form to help them through the slump. Being in form also gives you the chance to improve the chinks in your batting. It is always easier to incorporate new things when you don't have to worry about where the next run is going to come from. And perhaps that is what Sachin Tendulkar had been doing for the past two decades, constantly raising the bar and guarding against temptations and complacency.

INSIDE A DEBUTANT'S MIND

The sight of Simon Kerrigan bowling on day one of his Test debut made spectators stare at him in disbelief, then condemn his selection and later feel sorry for the poor lad. His cherished childhood dream, of playing for England, had turned into a nightmare on his first day at office.

The knowledge that many of his senior colleagues either boast Test centuries on debut, or remarkable bowling figures, must have weighed heavy too. That mindset of inflated expectations and fear of failure can affect a debutant horribly sometimes.

Kerrigan's first over went for ten runs; his next two included a huge full toss and a half-tracker that made him look woefully out of place. A stage as big as the Ashes can trigger a terrible chain of slip-ups, one leading to the next: a nasty trap with no exit.

On the one hand, the fantasy of playing for the country is so vivid and the visualization so real that you, as a debutant, can almost feel your teammates giving you high fives and the crowd standing up to applaud. On the other hand, you spend sleepless nights, twisting and turning, mulling over the possibility of being dismissed off the first ball, or getting hit for a four.

Days before the debut, you wear the team kit and stand in front of the mirror in the confines of your room, practising. While you are busy appreciating the gleaming national emblem stitched on your t-shirt, performance anxiety sneaks its way into your head. The cheers and applause you fantasized about earlier are replaced by murmurs and disapproval. Doubt makes an unwelcome appearance and pressure starts to make its presence felt.

Various thoughts circulate in your head: what if things go wrong, what if the ball doesn't come out right on to the bat, what if my feet don't move when the bowler delivers . . . The more you try to shoo them away, the stronger they become. You know that you must break the chain and sleep peacefully on the eve of the game, but that is the last thing that happens. The thought of realizing your dream keeps you awake, till exhaustion—emotional and physical—takes over and you crash.

Some top athletes are able to foresee this predicament and train themselves to deal with it. Indian Olympic gold medallist shooter Abhinav Bindra stayed up many nights in the run-up to the big event where he won the highest honours. He knew that sleep might desert him on the eve of the big final and so he meticulously prepared himself to perform in spite of a lack of sleep. As expected, he couldn't sleep the night before his big performance in Beijing, but that didn't affect his performance.

> Thoughts of 'what if things go wrong, what if the ball doesn't come out right from the hand, what if my feet don't move when the bowler delivers', start surfacing. The more you try to shoo them away, the stronger they become.

Sachin Tendulkar too didn't sleep well for about a fortnight leading into the match against Pakistan in the 2003 World Cup. If performance anxiety can keep seasoned sportsmen on edge, spare a thought for Simon Kerrigan, who was thrown into one of the most high-profile Tests of the year on debut.

For him, the morning of the match, the warm-ups, the presentation of the cap, must have all passed in a jiffy. And that is how life can be: one moment you are warming up, the next, you have a bat or ball in hand, practising your game, and then, before you have even absorbed the first few drills, the captains are out in the middle for the toss. One part of you wants proceedings to slow down so you can soak it all in, the other part, impatient and excited, wants to get it all over and done with as soon as possible. Then you are there, in the middle, 45,000 pairs of eyes watching your every move. In theory you are with ten other men of your clan; in reality you are alone.

I distinctly remember playing my first ball on my Test debut. Even though I felt reasonably well prepared, I prayed I would not get out first ball. A part of me felt paralyzed with anxiety. I am glad the other part was still awake and helped me take a single off the first ball. A monkey the size of a dinosaur was off my back. Looking back at it, what if I had played and missed for a while and hadn't got a single run off the first 25 balls? I am certain I would have melted under pressure and played a rash shot.

That was what happened to Kerrigan, unfortunately. Shane Watson, in an imperious mood, went after the debutant, and he didn't know how to react. A man who had bowled over 9,000 balls in first-class cricket and had taken 164 wickets ended up bowling chin-high full tosses and long hops.

It could possibly have been Kerrigan's worst-ever bowling spell at any level and unfortunately it came in the biggest match of his career, in front of a packed house. Stage fright took control of him and the dream turned into a nightmare in the space of twelve balls. His past stats showed that Kerrigan has been a much better bowler than what we saw on the first day at The Oval. Bowlers thankfully are able to turn it around, for they don't get only six opportunities in an over but also many overs to bowl in a match. However, that also means that you stand to be exposed many times over, as opposed to a batsman, whose misery might last only a few balls.

The great Shane Warne and many others have recovered from forgettable debuts. Simon Kerrigan would want to find consolation in that and the famous Zen saying, 'The arrow that hits the bull's eye is the result of one hundred misses.'

IN PRAISE OF THE OFF-SPINNER

If one were to ask ten lower-order batsmen (read bowlers) about the kind of bowling they would prefer to play, nine would instinctively say off spin. This helps explain why most playing XIs have just one off-spinner—if they have any, that is. When in November last year M.S. Dhoni decided to bring into play a two-pronged off spin attack, R. Ashwin and Harbhajan Singh, against England, it was the first such instance in a decade or so.

Traditionally, off spin has been the easiest form of bowling for a right-hand batsman to counter: the ball comes in after pitching and, even if you were to miss it in the flight or off the surface, you likely won't face the ignominy of getting stumped. You could be bowled if the ball sneaks through, but the option to use the body as a second line of defence gives most batsmen a sense of calm.

The first 'shot' that most kids learn to play is the slog in the direction of midwicket. This is ideally suited to off spinning deliveries, since one is hitting with the spin, reducing risk. Playing the away-going ball in the air with the spin requires a lot of skill, but even a No. 11 can slog with the spin effectively: a little bit of luck, bravado, strength and some skill, and the ball will sail into the vast vacant areas on the on side or into the stands.

With boundaries getting shorter, bats bigger and pitches flatter, off-spinners have had to reinvent themselves more than any of their other counterparts. Fast bowlers can bowl faster deliveries or radically reduce speed and thus create deception. Leg-spinners and left-arm spinners—the ones taking the ball away from right-hand batsmen—haven't had to invent new tricks to stay relevant because their existence hasn't been challenged as much as that of off-spinners.

Off-spinners have had to keep trying new things all the time in order to be counted. They have, by default or design, become one of the most forward-looking classes in cricket, always looking for options and defying batsmen, and it has done them good, for at one point it looked like they might become extinct. For instance, they are usually the first to go around the wicket to make sure the batsman has less room available to free his arms. While bowling around the wicket is widely considered a defensive option, off-spinners have managed to use it as a form of attack, maintaining an aggressive line by continuing to pitch it around the off stump. The easy option would be to pack the on-side field and finish on the batsman's legs, but they have mostly chosen to finish within the stumps to increase lbw possibilities.

It doesn't come as a surprise that in 2014's India–Australia Test series four off-spinners were employed—and effectively—by both sides. In fact, over the last six months, the leading off-spinners in the game today—Graeme Swann, Saeed Ajmal, Nathan Lyon, Glenn Maxwell, Mohammad Hafeez and James Tredwell—have all been called on to show their craft against India.

No longer just finger spinners, Muttiah Muralitharan changed the very description of an off-spinner. He wasn't your conventional off-break bowler who threw the ball as if turning a doorknob; he used his supple wrists and as a result started turning the ball more than any other finger spinner. In fact, he would turn the ball as much as the best leg-spinners did, if not more.

> The first 'shot' that most kids learn is the slog in the direction of midwicket. This is ideally suited to off-spinning deliveries, since one is hitting with the spin, reducing risk.

Murali's style of bowling forced batsmen out of their comfort zone, for stepping down the track wasn't an easy option anymore. In the past, batsmen could, using the body as a second line of defence, come down the track against off spin, for they only had to worry about the slider eluding them. Muralitharan's vicious turners started beating them on the other side too—the ball would spin across their bodies to offer stumping possibilities down the leg side. Even if the sweep and the slog sweep were plausible options, the extra spin off the surface would invariably take the ball a lot squarer than intended off these shots. Many batsmen were dismissed holing out at deep midwicket, targeting the vacant area between long on and deep midwicket.

The doosra

If Muralitharan's variety created confusion, Saqlain Mushtaq's ability to take the ball away from right-hand batsmen made them look like puppets. Saqlain took a leaf out of Muralitharan's book and, instead of bowling off spinners with the seam slightly tilted, bowled with a scrambled seam. While the flip side of not bowling with the seam tilted is a lack of consistency in the bite off the surface and the drift in the air, the positive is that batsmen are mostly unable to pick the spin in the air. Had Saqlain presented the seam to the batsmen, it would have been a lot easier for them to decipher the away-going ball just by looking at the seam position; not so with a scrambled seam.

Now the ball pitched within the stumps was no longer guaranteed to always head towards the batsman's legs. Saqlain's doosra, later employed by most off-spinners in the world, including Muralitharan and Harbhajan Singh, didn't just hold its line and go straight on but went the other way markedly, just like a leg-spinner's stock delivery would. This innovation made off-spinners a dangerous wicket-taking proposition.

The carrom ball

The latest trick in the off-spinner's bag is the carrom ball, bowled by flicking the fingers and propelling the ball out of the front of the hand. The ball follows a flat trajectory and goes away off the pitch, like a leg-cutter. Since much spin isn't imparted to the ball, it skids off the surface. Also, the flat trajectory means less bounce, and this in turn means it is difficult for the batsman to get under and find elevation. Additionally, the away movement makes on-side play even tougher.

Special mention must be made of Graeme Swann, who has managed to become one of the best spinners in the world without using the doosra and the carrom ball. Swann uses his long fingers and solid body action to generate spin off the surface and has mastered the slider, which holds its path instead of spinning into the batsman.

Off spin, whether orthodox or avant garde, by continuing to evolve and be effective and enchanting while fighting a battle for survival, deserves to be lauded.

INTRICACIES OF SETTING A FIELD

Picture this. The ball is turning square on a dry and crumbling Galle pitch. Muttiah Muralitharan licks his fingers, for he has already spun a web around the batsman. The batsman's legs are like lead, his mind frozen like ice. There is a slip, a short leg and a backward short leg to cash in on any mistakes. But why isn't there a silly point? A tentative prod off the front foot might just land straight into his lap.

There are many such field placements that make you wonder if something is amiss. Only later do you realize that all these fielding positions are part of a bigger plan.

Here the close-in fielder on the off side is missing because Murali wants the batsman to go right across and play a defensive shot on the off side. This is to entice him and give him the confidence that he can use the bat and not get out. Little does the batsman realize that trying to play the viciously turning ball against the spin is to flirt with danger, and it is just a matter of time before the inside edge flies towards close-in fielders on the leg side. Also, by not having a close-in fielder on the off, the bowler is also encouraging him to flirt with the doosra.

So, it is not only the fielders that matter, but also the spaces left vacant on purpose. It explains the fielding side's mindset and separates an ordinary captain from a brilliant one. Let us look over the play for field positions that almost always have a sub-text and hence makes the game even more interesting.

For fast bowlers

On the first day of the Test match, on a track with some juice in it, you would ideally start with a few slips and a gully. The distance from the bat and in between the slips fielders is decided by the bounce in the track. The lower the bounce, the closer the fielders to the bat and to each other. For instance, we stood almost 25–30 yards from the batsman in Australia and not more than 15 yards away at the Karnail Singh Stadium in Delhi to the same bowler, Ashish Nehra. The pace also dictates whether or not to leave the first slip vacant. On slow surfaces in the subcontinent, you could do without one, but on tracks like Perth you definitely need the area manned.

In seaming conditions, a short-leg comes into the picture straight away. His presence is not only to remind the batsman about the upcoming bouncer, but also to make him tentative while coming forward, for there is always a chance of an inside edge when the ball moves sideways upon pitching.

For an outswing bowler like Ben Hilfenhaus, the mid-off region is left vacant to entice a straight drive. Since the lines are always going to be slightly outside off stump—to bring the slip cordon into play and get the maximum movement—the batsman will have to play against the away swing to drag it down the ground; unless of course it is an over-pitched delivery within the stumps, which should be a rarity.

For an inswing bowler, the covers are mostly left unoccupied for a similar effect, to make the batsman play against the swing. The mid-on fielder would be a lot straighter for an outswinger and a little wider for the inswing. The idea is to force a shot against the swing.

Similarly on tracks with bounce and pace, like in Perth, the point fielder will be a lot finer. His role is not only to protect the area where more balls are likely to be hit, but also to reduce the amount of time the batsman has to react if he wants to score off that region. In effect, to score, the batsman will need to hit a lot squarer and hit slightly early.

On slow tracks, the fielders at point and square leg are a lot straighter. Since there isn't much pace to work with, it is quite a task to play finer.

The dynamics change if the pitch is flat and lifeless. Mid-on, mid-off along with extra cover and midwicket stand straighter to cut off the deliveries played with a straight bat. Since the bowler is trying to pitch the ball within the stumps, one of the slips makes way for added protection in the front. The square, though, is left vacant to lure the batsman into playing across the line.

Then there are people like Matthew Hayden who rarely play the squarecut. I have seen teams leave that position empty as a bait. Similarly for people who prefer to drive straight down the ground or fetch the ball from outside the off stump, like V.V.S. Laxman does, we have often seen fielders placed almost next to the non-striker.

We may not have seen batsmen getting out solely because of these innovative field positions, but men in these positions have caused many dismissals when batsmen try to do something off the cuff or take on the challenge to get past these fielders.

A silly-mid-off fielder is also an important position for a

quick bowler to play mind games, on tracks where he would want to push the batsman on the back foot. It is unsettling for a batsman to have a fielder like that in his eye line.

For spinners

Field placements for spinners make for an interesting study because spinners need to plan more elaborately; after all, a majority of their dismissals are through catches. Turning tracks bring about a lot of attacking field positions, while a flat track will have a mix of both attacking and defensive options. An off-spinner would happily leave the covers empty even when bowling outside the off stump. His idea is to entice the batsman to drive or cut against the spin and back himself to not bowl a half-volley or a half-tracker. But you will rarely see him remove the slip even if he doesn't bowl a doosra. He will retain it to keep the batsman guessing and to discourage him from playing too late.

Obviously the line of attack changes with the strategy in an ODI, where the priority is to save runs. The bowler pitches more towards middle and leg, so his field placements also change. A big turner like Murali would keep a short fine-leg, a square leg, and a mid-on in the circle, unlike someone like Ashwin who doesn't turn it much and hence prefers the long-on. All leg-side shots to Murali will go a lot squarer than intended so the region between deep midwicket and long-on needs to be manned. Unless you reach the pitch of the ball, all lofted shots will swirl towards that region. Also, in limited-overs, the field is mostly set with four on the off and five on the on side.

A leg-spinner or a left-arm spinner will choose his close-in fielders depending on the amount of turn he is extracting from the surface. The silly point is placed a lot straighter if there isn't much turn and is moved closer to the popping crease if the ball is spinning. A gully may also come into play if there is turn and some bounce. While a leg-spinner will prefer a short leg if he bowls googlies, the left-arm spinner will usually ask for the position only if there isn't much turn. And both will leave midwicket vacant if there is vicious turn.

When these bowlers go round the wicket and bowl in the rough, the field positions change dramatically. In setting the off-side field, they will play around the batsman's strengths. If the batsman likes to reverse sweep, they will have a point fielder, and if he prefers to step down the track to play inside-out shots, they will have the covers manned.

In Tests, the men who take the ball away from the batsman prefer a six–three off-side field. Surprisingly the same bowlers choose a four–five field in shorter formats because they are required to bowl within the stumps. Daniel Vettori would have a typical off-spinner's field while bowling to a right-hand batsman.

Setting in-and-out fields with close-in fielders in catching positions and others in the deep is another tried and tested strategy. The decision to keep the mid-on or mid-off fielder inside the circle will depend on which way the ball is spinning. The basic idea is to make the batsman go against the spin.

The play of fielders around the park is an intrinsic part of the act of setting up a dismissal. A batsman could use it as a clue to decipher the bigger plan, but he must tread with caution, for firstly it could be a trap to make him try different things and secondly, if he gets too absorbed in the setting of the field, chances are, he will play into their hands.

WICKETKEEPING

It isn't odd that a world charmed by aggressive batsmen, daunting pacers and incisive spinners often looks through the men crouching behind the stumps, playing singular roles for their teams. A wicketkeeper is usually the most underappreciated of the playing XI, constantly called upon to make vital contributions as a matter of routine. While a brilliant piece of fielding is usually praised when it occurs in the outfield, it simply is expected behind the wickets.

Nevertheless, wicketkeepers are the backbone of a fielding unit and are in the thick of the action through a game. The stronger the backbone, the tougher the team appears on the field. The keeper leads his team in setting the tone for energy levels and body language. Since he is closest to the batsman, his job is to convey the team's mood to the opponent, and of course, to intimidate him.

While it may be the most gruelling task on the cricket field, wicketkeeping is also a thankless job. You could be at your best behind the stumps the whole day, but the big gloves will take half the credit, and if, God forbid, you drop a catch, you can almost see your world coming down. A keeper's span of concentration—the amount of time he needs to stay in the present—has to be longer than that for other players. It starts with the bowler's run-up (when the keeper looks for cues with regards to the shine, or for any other indication that might help him move better) and ends when the ball is dead. To this mental effort, add 540 squats, ninety trots of about 50 metres each and about 200 short sprints every day.

They say wicketkeepers are born, not made. The craft chooses its disciple, not the other way around. Good wicketkeepers are blessed with great (read soft) hands, sharp reflexes and the right temperament.

Though it isn't a rule of thumb, and there have been exceptions, good wicketkeepers are also not very tall. Since a shorter person's centre of gravity is lower, it is easier for him to go down, and also to stay low on every ball, without too much effort. Taller guys, like Adam Gilchrist, have to remind themselves to stay low all the time.

In recent times, wicketkeeping has ceased to be a specialized job, the need of the hour being wicketkeeper-batsmen. While this may add depth to batting line-ups, it may, unless monitored closely, irreversibly alter the art of keeping—the one that requires the keeper to tweak his responses to different kinds of bowlers and balls bowled.

Keeping to spinners

If wicketkeeping wasn't already tough, standing up to the stumps requires special skills. The ideal stance of a wicketkeeper is one that gives him a full, uninterrupted view of the bowler. His inside foot (the one closer to the stumps) is about five centimetres outside the line of off stump and about two feet, or an arm's distance, behind. How far back he is from the stumps depends on the height of the player. The smaller the keeper, the closer he will need to be to the stumps.

While standing back to a medium-pacer, he can remain in a half-squat position, but he has no choice but to crouch fully while standing up to the wicket. The reason for staying crouched is to delay getting up for as long as possible, for it is easier to move upwards than down.

The keeper must start rising only after the ball has pitched, and must then move with the bounce. If he gets up earlier, he will invariably find himself in an awkward position, especially on low subcontinental wickets—a problem faced even by the best in the business, like Ian Healy or Mark Boucher in India and Sri Lanka. India's Nayan Mongia was as good as it got while standing up to the spinners. He would not only stay low for the longest possible time but also rise with the ball beautifully, even on India's uneven pitches, even while keeping to the pace of Anil Kumble.

It is very important to have the gloves fully unfurled while taking the ball. Snatching at the ball is a no-no. 'Receiving' is the operative word. While the palm closer to the stumps should be in line with the ball, the outer palm must cover the possibility of an outside edge. Since wicketkeepers are taught to keep their hands this way, it is unfair to be harsh when they miss inside edges, especially against spinners, because of the lack of time to rearrange the hands.

The head should be in line with the ball as you move sideways to collect the ball. Previously wicketkeepers used to be told to make an arc with the hands while moving sideways; this is now discouraged since it takes them away from the stumps. Now the advice is to move in a straight line while keeping the inside leg as close to the stumps as possible in order to get back to the wicket when needed.

For a keeper, reading the bowler is as important as it is for a batsman. It gives him clues regarding the direction of the ball and helps him decide which way to move. For example, there is no need to move down the leg side for a doosra pitched around middle stump, or to stay on the off side for a googly.

Keeping to fast bowlers

Although standing back is slightly easier than standing up, when standing back the wicketkeeper is also responsible for his teammates in the slip cordon. He is the one who decides the distance from the stumps—which should ideally be the spot at which he receives a ball pitching on good length at about waist height. If the ball gets to him higher or lower, it means he is not in the correct position. And since the fielders at slip use the keeper as an indicator for bounce and pace, if he is not in the correct position, they won't be either.

The keeper's position should be such that he gets a full, uninterrupted view of the bowler, which means he has to place himself further outside the off stump for bowlers coming around the stumps. In such instances you need to be a bit lenient if a keeper misses one down the leg side, for he has to cover a lot of ground to gather the misdirected ball.

It isn't mandatory to crouch fully but most keepers prefer to do so. There are some exceptions, like Alec Stewart, who liked to stay in a half-squat position. But keeping the knees flexed, with your weight on the balls of the feet, is mandatory and you should be able to move sideways in a straight line. The idea is to take the ball beside the inside hip and cover the outside edges.

Wicketkeepers are also advised to 'give' while receiving the ball, which means taking the arms back, using them as shock absorbers, while taking the ball. Though it is the right thing to do, it doesn't work in England, where the ball tends to swing a fair bit after passing the batsman. Gilchrist found that out in the 2005 Ashes and was clearly flustered in the first half of the series. In England you need to gather the ball in front of the body, using the body as a second line of defence.

A wicketkeeper must also go for every catch that is not likely to reach first slip on the full. It is better to get a hand to the ball and drop it than to not attempt to catch at all.

Keeping to the batsman

It is also the wicketkeeper's job to get under the batsman's skin. I am not promoting sledging but a bit of banter is harmless. Trust me, when someone stands that close to you—with the best view of play—and repeats things about your technique with confidence, you tend to give it a thought. And that fleeting thought might just be enough to force a false shot. I have been tempted to play a few myself, and have seen many batsmen fall for wicketkeepers' utterances. Parthiv Patel coerced Yasir Hameed into playing ahead of himself a few times on India's tour to Pakistan in 2003-04.

Since the wicketkeeper has the best view in the centre to judge the ball's movement, pitch quality, a batsman's strengths and weaknesses, the bowler's mistakes, he must think and act like a leader. He is a constant source of information for the captain and the bowlers.

A smart keeper brings immense value to the side: Stewart stumping Brian Lara with a smart piece of work and Brendon

McCullum moving down the leg side to pre-empt Rahul Dravid's paddle sweep to dismiss him are two examples off the top of my head. There are many such instances where keepers have played a pivotal role to change the course of a game.

A good wicketkeeper also makes the team look like a better fielding unit. He may run up to the stumps urging the players to throw at him, even when the batsmen are not attempting a run; he might run up to collect a bad throw on the full or collect a poor throw cleanly. He possesses the power to boost the spirits of the team and keep the players on their toes.

The keeper is the second-most important man in the side after the captain. One can almost discern the mood of the team just by looking at him.

PANIC vs CHOKE

Every time South Africa gets knocked out in a world event the c-word comes out again. Nothing seems to have changed for them in big tournaments ever since they came back to international cricket after the apartheid era. They have always had the arsenal to go all the way and yet have fallen short, always in the knock-out stages.

While their record cannot be contested, whether they choked or not in every such game can be debated. There is a fundamental difference between choking and panicking, which the writer Malcolm Gladwell explains quite proficiently. Although Gladwell talks in the context of tennis, his theory explains choking in cricket too.

What happened to South Africa against New Zealand in Mirpur in the 2011 World Cup was a bad case of panic, though it was conveniently considered a choke. So what exactly is choking and how is it different from panicking?

The fundamental difference is that while you think too much when you choke, you think too little when you panic. While choking, you want to delay the inevitable, but when you panic you want to get over with it as soon as possible, for you can't handle the growing pressure.

What constitutes choking?

You play safe

You may finish 30 runs short of the target if the opposition bowls really well and you lose all your wickets in the bargain. On the other hand, if you get to the fiftieth over needing 40 runs with 5 wickets in hand, that is more of a problem. Some may call it a miscalculation but it really comes down to the mindset: to play safe for as long as possible.

South Africa have done this more times than any other team. Remember the tied game against Australia in the 1999 World Cup when Allan Donald was run-out? The match would have finished much earlier had the Proteas not allowed Mark Waugh to bowl a lot of overs in the middle.

Chasing a target is a lot about identifying threats and weak links in the opposition and then treading with caution against potential threats while going after the weak links. Playing in safe mode can take you only so far; you must change gears at some point.

You don't take calculated risks

Yuvraj Singh could easily have dabbed the ball towards third man instead of going over the point fielder against Brett Lee in the quarter-final of World Cup 2011 in Ahmedabad. Going aerial may look dicey to some but it is extremely important to take calculated risks when you are playing against a strong opposition. If you wait forever for things to happen, chances are you won't be there when they do. When you refuse to take these calculated risks, you run the risk of digging a hole for the team, i.e., choking.

You think too much

'When thinking goes deep, decisions go weak.' This is an old saying that describes choking perfectly. Sport is more about instinct than intellect. Intellect is the primary requirement while planning but once the game starts, instinct must take over. You are more likely to succeed when you react, not over-think, for there is hardly any time to think too much.

When you overthink, you tend to worry about how things can go wrong and so you stop trusting your instincts. When you think before every step you take, you end up walking too slow. If you keep thinking about the possibility of getting stumped, you will never be able to go down the track.

Playing an aggressive shot is, most often, about backing yourself and trusting your instincts to go through with it. But the fear of what may happen if the shot is mis-timed, or if the ball bounces a bit more or less than expected, can result in a defensive prod. This is choking at a micro level.

I have also found that teams and individuals who are more inclined towards technique than flair are more likely to choke. Their strategic and technical know-how tell them to play it safe. On the contrary, people who have a healthy mix of technique with flair—say, a team like Pakistan—are less likely to choke.

What constitutes panic?

You commit hara-kiri

Panic is, in fact, the exact opposite of choking. If you play it too safe for too long when you choke, you self-destruct in fast-forward when you panic. What happened to South Africa in Mirpur was a classic example of panic. There were no demons in the track and the New Zealand attack wasn't all that formidable. South Africa were cruising at 108 for 2 at the halfway stage but once they lost a couple of wickets, panic set in. When you start trying to take non-existent singles (the A.B. de Villiers run-out), start manufacturing shots when you only need to play percentage cricket (J.P. Duminy's dismissal), play reckless strokes despite having a set batsman at the other end (Dale Steyn's and Robin Peterson's dismissals), it is a sign the team has lost it.

You abandon rational thought

You think too much while choking and too little when you panic. You may need to score a run a ball, but somehow it feels a lot more than that. A couple of dot balls are followed up by a high-risk shot to ease the pressure. When you panic you tend to overestimate the pressure. A run a ball, with wickets in hand, is like walking in the park on most days, but not when you are panicking. Rational thinking deserts you the moment you panic.

Why do teams play silly shots when wickets were tumbling all around them? It is common sense that if you are four down for not many, you must drop anchor, but they did exactly the opposite and tried playing ambitious shots. A six or a four can't win you the game, but you don't think along those lines when you panic.

Fear takes over

When you choke, you fear making mistakes and subsequently you fail. When you panic, it is the prospect of failure that you fear, which leads to committing mistakes. The fear of failure cripples you so much that you self-destruct and bring about the failure you fear.

Panic has a domino effect. It is like an epidemic that spreads through the team, while choking can be restricted to a couple of batsmen in the middle. Once panic sets in, it is quite apparent and visible to everyone, including the players in question, but choking goes unnoticed till the eventual calamity is at the door.

If I may draw an analogy from tennis: when a player chokes, he keeps hitting safe shots, bang in the middle of the court, ensuring they miss the net and are well inside the baseline, hoping the opponent will make a mistake. When the same player panics, he goes for non-existing winners, resulting in unforced errors.

The outcomes of choking and panicking may be the same but both are different from each other. So the next time you see a team lay down their arms, it might be worth looking closely to see if they have choked or panicked under pressure.

WHY IT PAYS TO BE A LEFT-ARM QUICK

Men like Trent Boult, Mitchell Starc, Mitchell Johnson, Wahab Riaz, Mohammad Irfan and Rahat Ali made the 2015 edition of the World Cup truly spectacular. These bowlers, with their left-arm pace, played a pivotal part in taking their teams through to the final eight. In a tournament—and a game—that has become very friendly for batsmen, left-arm fast bowlers have added a whole new dimension.

If there's a bowler who can make the batsman change tack before a ball is bowled, it has to be a left-arm fast bowler bowling over the stumps. When a right-hand batsman is facing a left-armer bowling over the wicket, he needs to open up his stance a bit; otherwise the point the ball is delivered from creates a blind spot him.

A right-arm fast bowler can achieve this too, when he goes around the stumps, but no matter how close a right-armer tries to come to the stumps, he'll never be close enough; and when the ball is delivered from wide of the crease, as in these instances, it simply can't pitch within the stumps and still hit the wicket. That rules out one major mode of dismissal: the lbw. Also, the ball bowled by a right-arm fast bowler from around the wicket is unlikely to swing back enough into the right-hander: the angle is simply too acute. On the other hand, the left-arm fast bowler doesn't face any such issues since the bowling arm is a lot closer to the stumps, and the moment it starts swinging back into the right-hander, the problems multiply for the batsman. That is where Starc and Boult have scored over the rest.

If it's only angling away, you can manage by planting the front foot across and playing outside the line every time. But as soon as one ball darts back in, you need to rethink and realign. Now you must not commit too much or else the incoming ball will have you in a tangle. A short front-foot stride is a must to the ball that's swinging back in. But the problem is that it's a given that some balls will hold their line and not come back in. The only way to gauge if the ball is going to swing or not is to keep an eye on the position of the seam and watch it in flight to figure out if the seam is wobbling or not. If the seam is facing leg slip and it's coming down bolt upright, you ought to assume that it's going to swing in. None of these methods are foolproof though. It happens for the right-arm fast bowlers too but the lack of angle there makes it easier for the batsman to handle the lack of swing on some deliveries; with a left-arm fast bowler, these balls often find the outside edge.

Left-arm fast bowlers have another inherent advantage over their right-arm colleagues because the angle that they create buys them some time and keeps the batsman quiet. Even if the ball isn't swinging in the air and the pitch isn't offering anything, the ball going across the batsman ensures that playing on the up isn't as easy as playing through the line to right-arm fast bowlers. While facing a left-arm fast bowler, the ball is always going away from you, and that sows the seeds of doubt.

It goes without saying that about 80 per cent of batsmen and bowlers in the world are right-handed, and therefore are used to batting and bowling against those of their kind. Familiarity breeds ease, if not contempt, in this case. Picture Wahab Riaz, who has a slightly tilted wrist at the point of release, which takes ten out of ten balls away from the right-hander, but still the angle is enough to fool even the best in the business.

I also think that it's easier to set fields to left-arm fast bowlers bowling over the stumps, simply because playing across the line to balls bowled at that angle is flirting with danger. These days, getting hit is inevitable for a bowler, and the only way to minimize the damage is to make sure that you decide where the batsman hits you. For a right-arm bowler, it's almost mandatory to man both sides because anything finishing within the stumps can be hit through the on side, and if you bowl outside off, the option for the batsman to walk across opens up too. The only way for the right-arm fast bowler to stop the batsman from doing this is to swing the ball away from him, but this doesn't always work when the ball is old. A left-arm fast bowler doesn't have such issues, for nine out of ten times the right-hander will target the off side against them: since the angle is taking the ball away, it seems prudent to play with it instead of against it. Finally, their natural variations give left-armers a head start in the death overs too. There are only three lengths that should be targeted in the death overs: bouncer, yorker, and the back-of-good-length for the heavy ball. The first two, when bowled by a left-arm bowler over the wicket are difficult to get away. As a batsman, you're taught that you shouldn't hook or pull the balls that are going away from you, for it's tougher to drag them in and still control them. Yorkers also pose a similar threat if they are going away from you, for the main target area for the batsman in the death overs is midwicket or long on, and to hit there, you must hit against the angle.

A lot of right-arm fast bowlers try to exploit that angle too in the final stretch of an innings, but when they do so, their slower delivery loses potency. The easiest slower one to bowl is the off-spin variety, and for a left-arm fast bowler that delivery automatically goes away from the right-hand batsman, which isn't the case with the right-arm fast bowler: he must develop a back-of-the-hand slower one or a leg-spin variant, neither of which is easy to acquire. Also, since their bowling arm is so wide on the crease, these variations are difficult to execute properly. Starc is phenomenal in the death overs for these very reasons—first the angle, then the reverse swing tailing away at the end, and finally the off-spin that goes away from the right-hand batsman.

If pitches across the world keep getting flatter and the one-day rules stay as they are, it won't be surprising if a left-arm fast bowler becomes mandatory in every playing XI.

PLAYING REVERSE SWING

Post the controversy surrounding Dhoni's unhappiness with curator Prabir Chowdhary, Kolkata's Eden Gardens had sprung a surprise for many of us who believed it would help the spinners during the third Test between India and England in 2012. Instead, fast bowler James Anderson proved to be the giant-killer with his persuasive reverse swing.

Conventional wisdom has it that the inswinger is the most lethal delivery when the ball is experiencing some reverse swing and that clean-bowled and lbw are the two most common modes of dismissal when that happens, especially for right-hand batsmen. When the old ball starts reverse swinging, the toughest delivery to play is the one that tails back into the right-hander, for nothing in the flight of the ball (except the shine, if you see it) suggests that the ball will dart back in at the last moment.

If one half of the ball is extremely rough and the other is shiny, even a trundler can generate reverse swing, but it won't be half as effective as what a genuinely quick bowler would produce. The slower the pace, the earlier the ball swings in the air; and the later the movement in the air, the tougher it is to handle.

To delay swing, all good bowlers bowl an inswinger as they would an outswinger, and vice versa. This basically means that the bowler will use the same seam position, wrist position and overall action as he would for an outswinger. In fact, he will also bowl it as an outswinger, pushing the ball towards the off side. Only when it loses a bit of pace—and the quicker you bowl, the later it loses pace—does it tail back in. The likes of Waqar Younis and Wasim Akram mastered this art.

Bowlers with slightly lower bowling arms create more problems than the ones who bowl with a high-arm action. That also explains why Anderson was more effective than Steven Finn in Kolkata, or why the likes of Lasith Malinga and Waqar have been more dangerous than Glenn McGrath, Javagal Srinath and so on.

The first and most trustworthy giveaway while countering reverse swing is to look for the shiny side of the ball. This isn't always a completely accurate indicator because every now and then the ball will misbehave, but when it starts reverse swinging, by and large it always moves towards the shiny side. So if you manage to see the shine, you can generally set yourself up a fraction in advance. This means opening the stance up a bit if the shine is facing midwicket (for a right-hander) and issuing yourself a mental warning not to fish outside off if the shine is facing covers. It isn't always possible to spot the shiny side, though, for good bowlers also master the art of hiding the shine while running in. Waqar and Wasim managed to hide it till the very last moment, which made them even more lethal.

Since you don't have much of a clue about the ball's final destination, it is important to resist the temptation to play the lines and instead to delay your movement till the last instant. This means that even when the ball is outside the off stump in its flight, you are best off not taking the front foot too far across—once you have committed to the shot, it will be impossible to bring the foot back in if the ball dips back at the last moment.

> The ball comes back in a lot more than it goes away when it is reversing, so most batsmen try to play inside the line at all times. While that takes care of the balls coming in, it leaves you vulnerable to those that hold their line or go away.

For some reason, the ball comes back in a lot more than it goes away when it is reverse swinging, so most batsmen try to play inside the line at all times. While that takes care of the balls coming in, it leaves you vulnerable to those that hold their line or go away fractionally. That is what Anderson exploited on day one in Kolkata in December 2012—he used the inswinger almost as a decoy of sorts to induce outside edges with the balls that held their line. Both Virat Kohli and Sachin Tendulkar were the victims of this strategy.

Another way to deal with reverse swing is to shorten your backlift considerably: the higher the backlift, the tougher it is to dig yorkers out. Tendulkar appreciably diminished his backlift against Anderson on day one. However, while this strategy can help keep the toe-crushers out, it adversely affects shot-making ability because of the lack of momentum.

While a short forward stride is recommended while countering reverse swing, it is important to not mistake it with not moving the feet at all. In order to counter any kind of lateral movement, be it off the pitch or in the air, it is imperative to use the feet decisively to get into the right positions.

Just like getting the ball to reverse swing effectively is a craft, playing it efficiently is one too—one that calls for a lot of skill and a stroke of luck.

PLAYING SPIN

Haven't we heard a zillion times that batsmen from the subcontinent are not comfortable against quick bowlers on bouncy tracks? A lot of Indian batsmen received flak during the whitewashes in England and Australia for their inability to handle pace and swing. But are the same experts and critics equally harsh on overseas players who are found wanting while handling spin on the subcontinent? Isn't playing the turning ball as difficult an art to acquire as handling short-pitched stuff? I definitely think so. Don't believe me? Ask Ricky Ponting about his horror series in India in 2001.

Playing the turning ball on a spiteful pitch needs not only technical prowess but also a certain amount of decisiveness in terms of foot movement and courage in shot selection. Not that the slow bowler can hurt you physically, but the mental scars, at times, are more difficult to heal.

This chapter is an attempt to outline the basics of playing spin bowling effectively.

Reading it from the hand

The reason most English batsmen struggled against spin for the longest time was that they were told to play the spin off the surface. Instead of trying to read the spin from the bowler's hand, they waited for the ball to pitch before setting themselves up, which was obviously way too late—though they did manage if the ball spun in the expected orthodox manner, i.e. from leg to off for a leg-spinner and off to leg for an off-spinner. But the moment the bowler bowled a doosra or a googly, they were at sea.

On the contrary, batsmen from the subcontinent are taught to read the ball right at the time of the release. A bowler needs to deliver a doosra or googly in a completely different manner to his stock ball, and if picked at the point of delivery, the batsman is always better equipped to handle it.

It doesn't end there. The seam position after release tells a story too. The direction in which the seam is tilted gives you a fair indication of which way the ball will spin after pitching. The shine on the ball informs you a bit about which way the ball will drift and also if the bowler has bowled an arm ball. An off-spinner keeps the shiny side facing his palm for an arm-ball.

These may not be foolproof methods of reading spin, but isn't batting a lot about educated guesswork? Of course, all of this goes for a toss if you are playing a spinner like Muralitharan, who likes bowling with a scrambled seam; in which case you have to completely rely on your judgement at the point of release.

Playing late and using your feet

Your job doesn't end with managing to read the spin from the hand and drift in its flight. On the contrary it starts there. Just like while playing fast bowlers, you must allow the ball to come close to you and play as late as possible. Your foot movement needs to be decisive and distinct if you are to be a good player of the turning ball. Since the deviation off the pitch is far greater for a spinner than for a fast bowler, it is mandatory to get to the pitch of the ball to smother that movement. While getting to the pitch of the ball is always advisable, it is more practical against a spinner rather than a quick bowler.

Good players of spin also use the depth of the crease to good effect. Michael Clarke is one of the best players when it comes to using the feet. I watched him from close quarters (standing at short-leg) when he scored a century on his Test debut, in Bangalore.

The golden rule while stepping out is to wait for the bowler to release the ball, so that he can't alter his length or line. Another rule of thumb to use is to advance against balls that go higher than the eye level.

Body-weight transfer

Correct transference of body weight is absolutely crucial while playing the slower bowlers. Since there isn't any pace to work with, it is the transfer of body weight at the time of impact that generates power and timing. Playing on the up is rarely an option against spin bowling and hence the weight must go forward in the direction in which you intend to play the shot. Good body-weight transfer also ensures that you hit the ball along the ground and not in the air.

The importance of the hands

Contrary to popular belief, keeping the bat and pad together while defending isn't the best method. Yes, there shouldn't be any gap between the bat and pad, but the bat must always stay slightly in front of the pad for a proper impact. Keeping the bat beside the pad occasionally results in the bat being hidden behind the pad, and it also gives the impression that you didn't offer a shot.

> The golden rule while stepping out is to wait for the bowler to release the ball, so that the bowler can't alter his length or line. Another rule of thumb to use is to advance against balls that go higher than the eye level.

Another thing one must keep in mind while playing spinners, especially in the longer formats, is to keep the hands very soft. The top hand should hold the bat firmly, while the bottom hand should be there just to support. Soft hands will ensure that the ball doesn't carry to the close-in fielders.

Hands and wrists play a bigger role in manoeuvring spinners and putting the ball into gaps, as compared to playing the quick bowlers. Watching V.V.S. Laxman or Mohammad Azharuddin play slower bowlers was like watching a painter working his magic on a canvas. The lack of pace obviously allows them to work the ball around, but it is still an art.

Pushing the fielder back and sweeping

Being aggressive on rank turners is extremely important, because regardless of how solid your technique, pushing and prodding won't be enough to survive. Vikram Rathour, a brilliant player of spin at the domestic level, told me that you must take the aerial route to push the fielders back. Once the bowler employs a long on and long off, batting becomes a lot easier.

A lot of non-Indian players are taught to sweep spinners as much as they can. While sweeping is a good option to disrupt the rhythm of the bowler, you must also have other tricks in your bag. Matthew Hayden was one of the most ferocious sweepers of the cricket ball, but what made him dangerous was that he didn't shy away from using his feet. If the bowler knows that you only sweep, he varies his length and speed to make it tough. But once you start using your feet, along with sweeping, even good bowlers find it tough to negotiate. Brian Lara's epic series in Sri Lanka in 2001-02 comes to mind straightaway.

Playing the ball from the rough outside leg

Negotiating balls pitched in the rough is extremely tough for a couple of reasons. One, since the ball pitches outside the leg stump, there is a blind spot to deal with. Two, you can never be sure of the amount of spin when it pitches in the footmarks.

Virender Sehwag has a unique way of handling it. He stands in his stance with both his feet in the crease. He reckons that this allows him to make the length shorter and play the pull shot. Laxman, on the other hand, has a completely different method. He steps down the track frequently and gets to the pitch of the ball and he doesn't hesitate to play against the spin. But the majority of batsmen like to pad it away for as long as possible before trying an occasional sweep—normal or reverse.

A player is, more often than not, a product of his environment. If you are exposed to quick and bouncy tracks early, you will automatically become comfortable against pace. Similarly, if you play your entire cricket on dirt bowls, you will be at home against spin. But like Clarke, Hayden and Lara, you could also work your way towards mastering this craft.

PLAYING THE BOUNCER

They say that the bat is ruling the roost and soon, bowling machines will replace bowlers, for they are in the game only to be hit. But bowlers still have one weapon that even the best of batsmen don't like: the bouncer.

It is also something bowlers enjoy, because it offers them the rare chance of getting back at batsmen in what is almost always a batsman dominated sport.

So what does a batsman think about a bouncer while standing in his crease?

It is case-specific. While playing a swing bowler, like Bhuvneshwar Kumar, you are not too bothered about him bowling it short. Not that he can't or won't bowl a bouncer, but his strength is pitching the ball up and moving it away from the batsman. Also, with the pace and the bounce he generates (or the lack of them) he would have to bowl it really short to get it up at the batsman's head. And that would give a batsman enough time to adjust. So while facing someone like him, you would always be looking to get onto the front foot.

But if you are facing Shoaib Akhtar, bowling at 90 miles an hour, someone who relies heavily on bouncers to intimidate a batsman, you are always on guard. You start looking for little hints, like any acceleration in speed in the run-up, body language, or what happened on the previous ball. But you wouldn't expect him to take the ball away from the batsman off a good line and length, and that allows you to stay on the back foot.

Does the bowling action affect how easily the batsman picks the bouncer?

It does. People with neat actions are a lot easier to pick as compared to ones with unconventional ones. For example, a Brett Lee or a Glenn McGrath is easier to pick compared to a Lasith Malinga or a Shaun Tait. While facing Lee or McGrath you can trust your eye to pick up the release, you can also trust the bounce. Bowlers with high arm actions, who have to delay releasing the ball in order to bowl a bouncer, are relatively easy to pick. But while facing Malinga, you simply do not know. You watch the release, but whether it is delayed or not, it is very difficult to figure out from that angle. And to add to a batsman's woes, a bowler like Malinga doesn't get even bounce, thanks to his action.

The pitch

The quality of the pitch dictates the way bowlers bowl bouncers and how batsmen play them. On tracks with even bounce and pace, batsmen find it easier to handle short-pitched deliveries: they either duck under the ball or move away from the line while standing tall. But if the bounce is uneven, the dynamics of facing short-pitched balls change. You cannot afford to get into a squat because that makes you a target waiting to be hit if the ball doesn't bounce as expected. Since a lot of batsmen prefer ducking underneath the ball, they become vulnerable on these tracks.

Similarly, bowlers use bouncers according to the surface—fewer bouncers on tracks with reliable bounce and more of them with two fielders on the fence behind square-leg on pitches with dodgy bounce.

The psyche

All batsmen know that if they show any sign of weakness, a bowler will pounce on it. Batsmen also know that showing an interest in taking on the bouncer will invariably attract more bouncers. And similarly, a batsman who ducks underneath or sways away usually discourages the bowler from using it too often.

Depending on their strengths, batsmen choose their options. Matthew Hayden walks down the track to persuade the bowler to pitch it short, which is his strength. Rahul Dravid lets it go to the wicketkeeper, which in turn forces the bowler to pitch it up, much to Dravid's advantage.

Why do bowlers bowl bouncers?

a. *To intimidate*: In order to get under the skin of a batsman, a fast bowler must be intimidating. A bouncer happens to be a very important tool for this, along with his big follow-through and stare. This is an especially successful tactic against lower-order batsmen.

b. *As a set-up for the follow-up ball*: Jason Gillespie did this very successfully. He would bowl a few bouncers to push the batsman onto the back foot and then present an outswinger outside the off stump on a tempting driving line, to induce an edge.
c. *To get a dot-ball*: The bouncer is a difficult ball to score off and bowlers use it to restrict scoring, especially in the shorter formats of the game.
d. *As a wicket-taking option*: How often do we see two men stationed at the boundary line behind square leg and the batsman getting peppered with bouncers? The idea is to lure the batsman into playing a pull or a hook and getting a top edge.

Why are some people more comfortable against short-pitched deliveries than others?

The same reason why some people drive the ball better than others. People who are brought up on slow and low tracks are primarily front-foot players and hence find it difficult to get their body in the right position to play a bouncer. The right position would be to get inside the line while staying side on. Staying outside the line would mean fetching it from off side, and squaring on would force you to fend at the ball.

The pull and the hook are instinctive shots against the bouncer, and picking the length is the key to executing them perfectly. It is essential to have the right backlift (bat going higher than the bounce) and to get the body in the right position (inside the line of the ball) for one to be able to play these shots well.

A lot of people start off poorly against the short ball, but work their way through; those who can't, fail to make it to next level. Michael Bevan was one such player. On the contrary, Virat Kohli struggled against the short ball early on so much that even on dry and lifeless pitches bowlers didn't mind bouncing him out. But now, no one dares bowl a short ball to him, for he has mastered the art of countering them.

Does the helmet make a difference?

Of course it does. One feels a lot safer under the protection of the helmet, especially while playing an aggressive stroke. The batsman doesn't need to worry about the top edge smashing into the skull, or missing the ball completely, which makes him a lot bolder. The helmet, to an extent, has allowed certain players to ignore the importance of getting the technique watertight, which was mandatory a couple of decades ago. Whenever the ball hits the helmet—be it anyone—my respect for batsmen from yesteryears grows manifold.

I am assuming that most batsmen in those days would have preferred swaying away instead of ducking. But playing a defensive shot or letting the ball pass is one thing and playing a pull or hook without a helmet on is quite another. One needs to be 100 per cent technically correct every single time, because one mistake could be fatal. The batsman needs to not only trust his eye but also the ball to bounce as much as he expected. Hats off to batsmen like Viv Richards and Sunil Gavaskar.

How effective is the bouncer?

Theoretically, and perhaps also in reality, the bouncer is the only ball that can hurt the batsman physically (apart from the beamer, which is illegal, and a toe crushing yorker). But one way of looking at it is: what doesn't get you out doesn't hurt you. So even if most batsmen don't like facing the bouncer, they still prefer it over a good outswinger, which could take the outside edge. I am not saying you can't get out on a bouncer, but if you have a decent technique and are not afraid of getting hit, the chances of getting out are minimal.

We batsmen like to believe that the bouncer doesn't scare us, but from time to time it does. When you have made the wrong decision, like ducking underneath when the ball wasn't all that short, or when the bouncer keeps following you while you are trying to sway away, you are worried. I wouldn't call it a fear of the short ball or of getting hit, but the feeling of being vulnerable and helpless is unsettling. The moments just before the ball crashes into the helmet or your body feel a lot longer than they actually are. Everything moves in slow motion and you remember the gory details of the accident for a long time to come. And accidents, however rare, are scary.

PLAYING THE SWINGING BALL

While the world sat admiring Dale Steyn's swing bowling which caused India's capitulation in Nagpur in February 2010, the batsman in me couldn't help but feel sorry for our lot. Steyn was impeccable with his line and length, crippling even the best in the line-up. As he showed his calibre with a seven-wicket haul, I wondered if anybody spared a thought for how batsmen feel when the ball is darting around.

Why did Murali Vijay and Wriddhiman Saha shoulder arms when the ball was coming in? Why did Sachin Tendulkar play at the one going away only to nick it to the wicketkeeper?

It is harder to judge a swinging delivery than it looks. One, it requires a lot of guesswork. Even the most skilled batsmen in the world rely on their instincts and years of practice to gauge where the ball will end up when it reaches them. There is no device to tell you that the ball will move x inches in the air after release and y inches after pitching. And if the ball is moving at 145 km per hour, the time to assess becomes shorter and the margin of error even smaller.

There are certain things that a batsman keeps in mind while preparing to play the new ball. It helps if you have played the bowler in the past or if there is some video data to structure your game plan. If you are up against Matthew Hoggard or Brett Lee, who swing the ball away from the right-hander, you draw an imaginary line outside the off stump and leave alone all balls that pitch outside that line. In fact, you have to play well within that line to cover the movement in the air and off the surface. You can't play balls outside the off stump with a straight bat, for it doesn't cover for swing—you would probably end up nicking it to the keeper. You have to play with a slightly horizontal bat, which ensures that you cover the movement. A good example of covering for swing with a not-quite vertical bat would be Michael Vaughan's drive on the off side. In this case, the batsman is beaten only when the bounce is more or less than expected.

However, you will need to play with a straight bat when you are up against someone like Shane Bond, who swings it back into the right-hander. Not just that, you will also have to play late and close to the body to ensure there is no gap between the bat and pad.

Whether the ball is moving away or coming in, you need to constantly judge the amount of movement a bowler will get.

Be watchful of subtle changes in the bowling action, wrist and seam position and the bowler's use of the crease. Bond and Makhaya Ntini, who predominantly get the ball back into the batsmen, bowled from wide of the crease to use the angle. Outswing bowlers, on the other hand, prefer bowling from close to the umpire, for that allows them to start their line from the middle stump, to increase the chances of getting the batsman to play at it.

Then there are bowlers like James Anderson and Bhuvneshwar Kumar, who bowl close to the stumps and are still able to move the ball both ways. And if that wasn't hard enough to read, bowlers set batsmen up by bowling outswingers from the corner of the crease and inswingers from close to the stumps.

The wrist position is a good indicator of the way the ball will come out of the hand. Ishant Sharma tilts his wrist to push the ball inwards, while Zaheer Khan and Dale Steyn bowl with a straighter wrist, which allows them to swing the ball both ways.

Once the ball is released, the seam can reveal some more. It will be tilted towards the slip cordon if the ball is set to move away, and towards fine leg if it is going to come in. That is not a guarantee, though. I remember getting bowled by Jason Gillespie in the third Test against Australia in Nagpur in 2004. He bowled close to the stumps, his wrist was straight and the seam pointed towards second slip. So I expected it to move away and shaped myself for it, only to find the ball darting back in after pitching. I was bowled, and so was Rahul Dravid under similar circumstances. The only difference being that he managed to get an inside edge. On these occasions, you have to consider yourself unlucky, and in this case I wasn't the only one.

Another way of judging the path of the ball after release is to look for the shine. In case of traditional swing, the ball moves in the opposite direction to the side the shine is on; if the shine is on the right, the ball will move to the left and be an outswinger for a right-hand batsman.

> If you can't see the shine while playing reverse-swing, as a right-hander you need to be ready for incoming deliveries, because for right-handers it moves in more appreciably than away. Play inside the line to ensure that you cover the movement coming in. If it moves away, the most it can do is to beat the bat.

This is not guaranteed either. At times, the ball misbehaves and holds its line—which may not be as bad as it swinging in the opposite direction but still causes trouble.

To make life difficult, bowlers like Zaheer had mastered the art of hiding from the batsman which side of the ball is shiny. When the ball is reverse swinging it moves in the direction of the shine, unlike with conventional swing. If the shine is on the right, it will move towards the right, as an inswinger to the right-hand batsman. It is similar to traditional swing but the swing occurs a little late in the air. Good exponents of reverse swing have the ability to delay the swing till about a few feet before it lands. Most batsmen get duped into believing it is a straight ball till it darts in or out at the very last moment. The later the movement, the more difficult it is to adjust.

It is slightly easier to gauge if you can see the shine, but a lot tougher if you can't. That is when the non-striker comes to your rescue, since he is in a better position to see which side is shiny. He can't tell you outright, but his bat can. What he will do is hold his bat on the side of the shine—in his right hand if the shine is on the right and vice versa. But there are times he isn't sure, so he will keep the bat in the middle and you are left to deal with it by yourself.

If you can't see the shine while playing reverse swing, as a right-hander you need to be ready for incoming deliveries because for right-handers it moves *in* more appreciably than it moves *away*. Play inside the line to ensure you cover for the movement coming in. If it moves away, the most it can do is to beat the bat.

Bowlers like Mohammad Asif and Glenn McGrath rarely get the ball to swing in the air; they relied on movement off the pitch. There is little a batsman can do against these bowlers, at least as long as the ball is new and the shiny side is not visible. What you look for are subtle changes: does the non-bowling arm drop slightly earlier in the action? That may mean an off-cutter is on the way. If it is held on to till late, it is probably a leg-cutter. But again, it is difficult to be sure every time.

Playing the swinging ball is a tough proposition. Admire the batsmen who do it with aplomb and sympathize with those who struggle.

SECTION THREE

T20 CRICKET

BATTING

We have heard it ad nauseam: the T20 format belongs to batsmen. Bowlers are a lot like bowling machines, serving up balls to be hit to all parts of the ground. If you go by the number of runs being scored in T20 cricket and notice the economy rates of bowlers, you would side with that opinion as well. But let us look at this game from a batsman's perspective as well.

Does the quality of the bowling deteriorate in T20 cricket

No, it doesn't. But both good and great bowlers still go for plenty of runs because getting out—which scares the batsmen in other formats—is considered insignificant in T20. In an ODI, the top six or seven batsmen are supposed to bat fifty overs; so we see a conservative approach to batting, even in the powerplay overs. But there is no such responsibility in T20. In any case, one decent partnership is enough to consume the major part of twenty overs and then the rest of the batsmen can go completely berserk. It is astonishing to see the kind of shots batsmen—and in some cases even bowlers—pull off when they do not have the fear of getting out.

More time than it seems

Let us look at how batsmen prepare for and look at this format. Australia's David Hussey, a successful T20 player, says that there is more time in a T20 game than one thinks. When a batsman walks in to bat and knows that his team needs nine an over, the natural tendency is to become adventurous from the first ball. But it is not often that he can hit the first ball for a four or a six. Besides, attempting a big shot before he can see the ball properly would mean a greater risk of getting out and hence putting the team in further trouble. That is where Hussey's advice comes handy.

You should give yourself at least a couple of balls before exploding. You can always take a couple of singles to rotate strike and get the blood flowing in the veins. This, in turn, might also ease the pressure and help you assess the situation objectively. There are 120 legal deliveries to be bowled in every game and if you can reduce the number of dot balls, the pressure that comes from thinking you have been holding up the strike and need to hit a big shot is drastically reduced.

Balls at a premium

In Test cricket, the batsman gets a few overs to get his eye in, in a fifty-overs match he gets a few deliveries, but in T20 he should ideally take not more than a couple of balls. That is the reason why batsmen in the dugout are always padded up and glued to the game. Information is vital in a T20 game, and hence a batsman, after getting out, informs the remaining players how the track is behaving and what the par score would be. Most batsmen, while waiting for their turn to bat, also make a mental sketch of the areas they would target while facing certain bowlers.

> Twelve runs an over from the last three might sound extremely difficult, but 36 off 18 balls doesn't sound that ominous. If you can manage six hits to the fence in those 18 balls, you need only singles from the remaining balls.

Since balls are at a premium, players who can hit boundary shots are valuable. You can only go so far with just rotating strike; ultimately you should be able to clear the fence.

Calculated risk

While it is good to consume a couple of balls before going big, there are certain situations that demand a different strategy. For example, if your team is chasing over 160 runs, it is imperative to go after the bowling in the first six overs. In such cases the strategy of the fielding team is to form a ring and bowl on one side of the wicket, which makes piercing the field along the ground extremely difficult. That is why players like Brendon McCullum, Matthew Hayden and Virender Sehwag, who aren't scared of taking the aerial route, are more successful in the powerplay overs.

It is not easy to take singles when seven fielders are inside the circle; it is either a boundary or a dot ball. Batsmen who manage to play with the bowler's mind are also more successful than the rest. A.B. de Villiers is a prime example of this, for he moves so much while the bowler is getting ready to bowl that it is almost obvious to get confused. He would walk down the pitch, go across, go deep inside the crease or would go both across and deep inside the crease to force the bowler into bowling to his strengths.

Identifying the weakest and strongest links in the opposition bowling is important. For example, if it can be avoided, you wouldn't want to go after Muralitharan or Daniel Vettori in subcontinental conditions. And in seamer-friendly conditions you would like to play it a little safe against quick bowlers while targeting spinners.

A stable base, and staying away from the ball

Keeping a stable base is extremely important when hitting a long ball. Kieron Pollard, Andrew Symonds and Rohit Sharma are good examples of keeping a stable base and head while hitting the ball in the air. Most batsmen, including myself, are guilty of losing the shape of the shot when we try to manufacture shots or slog, which eventually ends up looking ugly.

Unlike Test cricket, where the batsman is supposed to use his feet to get close to the ball, the batsman is better placed if he stays away from the ball in T20 cricket. Staying away from the ball allows him to free his arms and also get under the ball to get elevation.

Go-to areas

Every batsman must identify his 'go-to' areas and shots, at least one each on both sides of the wicket. Once you have mastered these strokes, which could be over covers on the off side and over midwicket on the on side, you either wait for the ball that can be hit in those areas or make room or walk inside the line to create that shot. David Hussey says that one should back oneself, especially when it comes to hitting balls in his go-to areas. The idea is that if the first ball is bowled in your area you shouldn't be afraid to go for it.

Thinking in balls, not overs

Another thing that batsmen agree on is thinking in terms of the balls remaining, not overs. One must try to break it down even further. For example, 12 runs an over from the last three might sound extremely difficult, but 36 off 18 balls doesn't sound that ominous. If you can manage six hits to the fence in those 18 deliveries, you will only need singles from the remaining balls. Putting it that way makes it sound easier, yet we all know it isn't; but it surely is slightly less difficult than thinking in terms of scoring two runs per ball.

T20 has also taught batsmen to never give up. Even if the asking rate is fifteen runs an over in the last five overs, batsmen have started to believe that it can be achieved.

There can be a number of theories when it comes to batting in T20 format, but it boils down to how an individual reacts to the situation when he walks in to bat.

BOWLING

Traditionally bowlers tend to win Tests for teams, and batsmen ODIs. An offshoot of fifty-over cricket, T20 follows the parent format. T20 is perhaps even more about sixes than yorkers. While most who matter accept that T20 is a batsman's prerogative, how can one expect bowlers to remain unfazed? It is rather difficult to defend when batsmen come armed with a single motive, and without the responsibility of lasting fifty overs.

Bowlers who go for around five to six runs an over in ODIs consistently go for a lot more in this format. What stops batsmen from going after the bowling in an ODI is not only the quality of bowling but also the fear of getting out. The top six batsmen are supposed to bat fifty overs. In T20, however, there is no such burden on them and batsmen have the licence to go after the bowling right from the start.

Also, there is very little to choose between a Muttiah Muralitharan and a Yusuf Pathan in this format. On a given day, Yusuf, a part-time off-spinner, might be more effective than the man with the most Test wickets in the world. Respect for bowlers has therefore gone down remarkably. In Tests and

ODIs, batsmen would like to be cautious against certain bowlers and target the rest, but in a T20 bash you are almost forced to treat everyone equally. Every ball coming your way needs to be met with aggression regardless of who has bowled it.

So bowlers have gone back to the drawing board and chalked out a few ways to counter the assault they have been subjected to in T20.

Three lengths

For starters, fast bowlers have realized that only three lengths work in this format: yorkers, just short of good length and bouncers. Only in the first couple of overs, when the ball is swinging and the batsmen are slightly guarded, can a bowler get away with bowling any length other than the three mentioned above. In that early period one can try to pitch it up to the bat, hoping to take it away or bring it in to the batsman. But as soon as the ball loses its sheen, bowling full is considered criminal. Once the batsman has made up his mind to go on the offensive, it is mandatory to hit the desired length at will.

There are no half measures, as the margin of error is very small. A slight error in length turns an intended yorker into a half-volley or a full toss, resulting in a hit to the fence.

Yorkers, which were bowled mostly in the death overs in ODIs, are used liberally in this format. Earlier, yorkers were supposed to be directed towards the batsman's toes, but nowadays bowlers have also started bowling them outside the off stump. Players like M.S. Dhoni have found a way of hitting yorkers directed at their legs. They clear their front leg and make room to swing their arms. Bowlers have started going wide outside the off stump to counter that.

Change of pace

There is another skill that every seam bowler has tried to master: bowling the slower ball. Most bowlers practise different kinds of slower ones: from the back of the hand, the split-finger one, the traditional off-cutter, and some like Sreesanth have even tried bowling proper leg breaks. But more than the variety, it is the ability to bowl the delivery while under pressure and disguise it that makes it work.

The slow bouncer is a new addition to this category. Shaun Pollock started bowling it a long time ago, but there weren't many takers for it till recently. Now we see many bowlers using it to great effect.

Start well, finish well

Stats suggest that the first and last balls of overs are the most expensive balls in T20, and all bowlers now know the importance of starting and finishing an over strongly. The first and last balls, after all, make one-third of a bowler's quota in any format of the game. Starting an over strongly puts pressure on the batsman to do something out of the ordinary in the remaining five balls and finishing well reduces the pressure on the bowler bowling from the other end. That is what bowling in partnerships is all about, where both bowlers complement each other to create an impact.

> Bowlers have made peace with the fact that they are going to be hit, and that acceptance has led them to devise different strategies. Instead of trying to stop batsmen from hitting, bowlers try and ensure that batsmen can hit only in the direction they want them to hit.

No looseners

This brings us to the importance of keeping yourself warm and loose throughout the game. One can't afford to bowl a couple of warm-up balls to a fellow player because of the time constraints; you also can't afford to start the spell with a loosener. This is why bowlers, while standing at the boundary, bowl to their non-playing teammates or support staff, who stand with a baseball glove on, to assist them.

The single is the new dot-ball

In other formats only a wicket-taking delivery and a maiden are considered good deliveries, but T20 has widened the definition. A single conceded off a ball is considered as good as a dot ball in most situations. Bowlers know this and are seen giving singles after bowling a dot ball or two.

Go-to deliveries

Just like batsmen have their go-to shots, bowlers also master their go-to deliveries, which they rely on themselves to execute perfectly under pressure. They could be yorkers, bouncers or slower ones, which will bail them out in a tight situation.

Accepting the inevitable

Another interesting development is that bowlers have made peace with the fact that they are going to be hit, and that acceptance has led them to devise different strategies. Instead of trying to stop batsmen from hitting, bowlers try and ensure that batsmen can hit only in the direction they want them to hit. For example, if the bowler has set a heavy off-side field, he tries to bowl in areas from where he can't be hit towards the on side.

Sounds tough? Well, it is. Certainly for the bowlers. Didn't they tell you it is a batsman's game?

CAPTAINCY

Adam Gilchrist said that as the game is getting shorter, the role of the captain is getting bigger. Nothing could describe the T20 situation better.

Why is leading a T20 side different and more difficult than leading in other formats? Cricket played over five days or spread over two fifty-overs innings should logically be far more taxing than the slam-bang three-hour T20.

Well, it is true that T20 cricket defies logic time and again, for it isn't considered a thinking man's game. But that doesn't mean that you don't need to be smart to play it.

Not too long ago, just as this format was beginning to gain popularity, players tended to treat T20s like ODIs. In the fifty-over format the best bowlers are kept for the powerplay and the death overs, under the assumption that batsmen are most aggressive during these periods. The other bowlers are reserved for the middle overs, when the batsmen are expected to go a little easy. But when applied to T20, this strategy failed. With eight an over considered par, and the luxury of being able to lose ten wickets over twenty overs, batsmen remain on the offensive throughout.

Bowling changes

It is no longer mandatory to give your best bowler the first over. In fact, it is often smart to start with a part-time bowler, since most batsmen take at least a couple of deliveries to gauge the pace and bounce of the track. But you must know the batsmen's strengths and pick the bowlers accordingly. It wouldn't be a bad idea to start with an off-spinner against David Warner or Chris Gayle: both are known to be usually more comfortable against pace.

Also, you need to not get carried away by an economical first over, because the same bowler can go for plenty in his next. Batsmen tend to size up the bowler in his first few deliveries and mark their scoring areas for the next over. More often than not, the second over is more important than the first, so that should be bowled by your best medium-pacer.

Rotating your bowlers in the first six overs will work if your bowlers are comfortable bowling one- or two-over spells. Shane Warne and Rahul Dravid did it successfully for the Rajasthan Royals, often using up to five different bowlers in the first seven overs without letting the batsmen get away. It is like a game of chess, where you try to pre-empt the opposition's moves. At times you let the opposition score in the first six overs because you think it will be easier to pull things back once the ball gets old, and on other occasions you stifle the batsmen at the top to create pressure.

There are no foolproof methods to succeed, so you have to go with hunches. One wrong choice can change the momentum of the game. A captain makes more bowling changes in a T20 than he would in a fifty-over game. You can always recover from a bad over in an ODI, but in a T20 it is 5 per cent of the innings and can cost you the game.

In terms of bowling, captains also have to keep in mind the hefty fines they can be slapped with for slow over-rates.

Batting line-up

Deciding the batting order isn't easy in T20s. When do you send in your best striker? In IPL 2014, Delhi Daredevils simply couldn't find a way to efficiently use their in-form batsman J.P. Duminy and Mumbai Indians are regularly guilty of under-utilizing Kieron Pollard. For both these teams, their best strikers didn't get enough balls to make an impact. On the other hand, while it is tempting to give the big hitters the chance to get the most strike, it may not always be the wise option, for they might be ill-equipped to play the faster bowlers or the new ball.

The captain also has to pick the right overseas players for every game. He is usually spoilt for choice and it must be tempting to want players like Glenn Maxwell and Mike Hussey even when they aren't in form, and difficult to leave out someone like Dale Steyn.

Changing the field

The captain and the bowlers need to work out the fielding positions for every delivery: get third man inside the circle for a slower one, have mid-off in the circle for a bouncer. Bowlers need to assume leadership and the wicketkeeper and the fielders must chip in too, because it is hard for the captain to keep tabs on everything. The keeper is often assigned the role of getting the fielders in the right positions. We, at the Kolkata Knight Riders, were instructed to look at the wicketkeeper after every ball, for last minute instructions could come from that direction.

But there is still more to leading a T20 side, particularly in the IPL. You have to know and remember the strengths of all your players, understand their temperaments and predict how they will react to different situations in the middle.

The time-outs

We have seen teams lose momentum and falter after the breaks. Fielding captains can use the time-outs to their advantage—as the batsmen tend to take a few deliveries to get back into the groove—and slip in an over from a part-time bowler.

The teams that try to continue playing the way they did before the break often pay dearly.

I wonder if Yuvraj Singh or Virender Sehwag will really complain about having lost the captaincy of their IPL sides. It is certainly not an enviable job. Most captains will have aged a bit by the time the IPL ends.

PLANNING

Following the five World T20 tournaments, the seven seasons of the IPL and many other T20 matches, one would assume that teams and players would have identified a way of doing things in this format. Though some might argue that it is still a game of cricket and hence should not be treated any differently, people who play the game realize that all formats follow individual patterns, with a few variables here and there.

Initially T20 cricket was perceived as a twenty-over slog and most teams made the mistake of going too hard right from the beginning and hence losing wickets and their way.

Powerplay

Yes, there are field restrictions in the first six overs and one must try to take full advantage of them. But teams who lose more than two wickets in the first six overs more often than not seem to end up on the losing side. Hence the crucial question in this situation is: do you attack the bowling right from the start or keep a cautious approach while the ball is new?

Most teams have agreed that while they must capitalize on field restrictions, it should be achieved without losing too many wickets. Teams usually assign roles to the batsmen in the middle, as part of strategy. For example, in the first IPL, we at Kolkata Knight Riders gave Brendon McCullum the licence to go berserk in the first six, while the batsman at the other end was supposed to make sure McCullum got majority of the strike. If McCullum got out, the team would send another hitter and a grafter in case the other batsman lost his wicket.

Bowlers also have designated roles to play. Ishant Sharma, and briefly Shoaib Akhtar, were allowed to go for a few runs in the first six overs in order to take wickets.

Conditions

The way a team approaches the first six overs depends a lot on the playing conditions.

In the Indian subcontinent, the new ball doesn't move around much, hence the risk of getting out is relatively smaller than in South Africa, England or Australia, where the conditions are different.

Secondly, once the ball gets old, it starts gripping the surface, and it gets tougher for batsmen to clear the fence consistently. So the order of the day in such circumstances would be to maximize the first six overs.

On the other hand, barring the worn-out South African pitches in the second edition of the IPL, and slow tracks in the West Indies, batting becomes easier on most pitches in the rest of the world as the game goes on. So a more cautious start would be the more viable option in those cases.

Strengths

Teams play to their strengths. Some are top heavy and some rely on their hard-hitting batsmen to finish the innings on a high. In IPL-7, teams like Chennai Super Kings (with Dwayne Smith and Brendon McCullum) and Royal Challengers (with Chris Gayle) relied on capitalizing on the field restrictions, while teams like the Mumbai Indians didn't mind a slow start, for they had Pollard and Corey Anderson to finish things off.

> Once the ball gets old in subcontinental conditions, it starts gripping the surface, and it gets tougher for batsmen to clear the fence consistently. So the order of the day in such circumstances would be to maximise the first six overs.

The middle overs are utilized to either carry on the momentum or to build a platform for one final assault in the final four overs. Matches are neither won nor lost in these middle overs—high-scoring games being an exception. It is unreal how many runs teams manage to score in the last three to four overs if they have wickets in hand.

Chasing or setting a target

The strategy for chasing a target differs from the one followed while batting first. Teams can afford to leave it until late in the innings if they are setting a target, but while chasing they must keep tabs on the asking rate, or else one economical over can change the equation.

Being realistic

T20 cricket has forced bowlers to shed their pride. Now you

see the wicketkeeper standing up to almost all medium-pacers—which a lot of bowlers used to consider an insult till recently—to prevent batsmen from walking down the track. Only the really quick men can afford to have the wicketkeeper far behind throughout their spell. And even they have started placing third man inside the thirty-yard circle while bowling slower deliveries and yorkers on the leg stump. The chances of the ball going towards third-man are minimal with both those deliveries if executed properly.

Taking responsibility

Kolkata Knight Riders and John Buchanan were criticized by all and sundry for the multiple-captain theory, but if applied properly it isn't such a bad idea. Every captain and coach encourages his players to think and act as a captain. Batsmen, since they are always alone in the centre, are used to doing this. The endeavour is to also encourage bowlers to think along the same lines. With the pace at which this format runs, the bowler should not be expecting the captain or anyone else to adjust the field, but should take the lead and do it themselves.

To be honest, I don't think there is what you can call a set winning strategy or a pattern in this format. While the players continue to find their feet in this latest off-shoot of traditional cricket, it is perhaps the absence of a predictable pattern that continues to attract people to T20.

THE SCIENCE OF BIG HITTING

All batsmen hit the ball to score runs but some build their games around hitting big and hard. Glen Maxwell and Chris Gayle belong to that category, while Jacques Kallis looks to find a balance between aggression and defence. I am not a big hitter, so I watch in awe when someone like Maxwell or Gayle goes berserk.

But there is more to hitting the ball hard and far than just whacking a white round object thrown your way. There are different ways to hit the ball and this is my attempt at breaking up the method behind the madness. (Though it would have been better if I had cracked it when I played for India.)

Momentum

To play fast bowlers behind the wicket, you can use the pace of the ball to good effect. But if you want to hit them down the ground it is almost like playing against spinners: you will need to generate some pace of your own. In other words, find some momentum, something which can be achieved in different ways.

The backlift: The higher the backlift, the harder the impact of bat on ball. That is why we see players like Yuvraj Singh and Virender Sehwag hitting further than the rest without really trying to knock the leather off the ball. To get the bat to come down at the right time, they need to either initiate the downswing early or increase the bat speed; but those are small adjustments to gain the extra yards. Many Australian batsmen, like Ricky Ponting, cock their wrists at the highest point of the backlift to get the bat higher, and then unwind at the point of impact. That increases the backlift and the bat speed.

Use your feet: Most batsmen prefer this to adjusting their backlifts. The objective here is to throw the weight of the body behind the shot at the point of impact. It is common to step out of the crease against the spinners—Sourav Ganguly does it really well, especially against left-arm spinners—but these days many batsmen successfully do it against fast bowlers as well.

Timing

Players like Sachin Tendulkar are blessed with this gift. They don't need high backlifts to send the ball speeding down the ground or careening through the air. The trick is to meet the ball at the right point of the downswing and then transfer the weight from one foot to another at the point of impact. It is as complicated as it sounds and that is why a lot of good batsmen spend their careers searching for this elusive skill. And it is why less-accomplished batsmen, despite high backlifts and powerful arms, rarely manage to clear the fence.

Maintaining shape

Hitting a long ball on a regular basis is as technical as playing a cover drive. While the backlift and downswing are important, the shape a batsman maintains during and after the shot is equally important. Gayle is a good example: he keeps his head still and maintains a stable base and good shape, during and after the shot. No wonder he is one of the biggest hitters of the ball. The follow-through, a by-product of a good downswing, is just as important. The arms should follow the line of the shot and not fall away.

Free your arms

You must have room to swing your arms freely. Bowlers will try to eliminate this space by pitching it straight, and batsmen respond by clearing the front leg to create the necessary room—Suresh Raina does it to hit the ball in the midwicket area—or by going deep inside the crease to get under balls that are pitched up. M.S. Dhoni is really good at getting under the ball and that is why he manages to hit yorkers with ease.

If you want to hit in the air, there are some more things to keep in mind.

When you step out, you must not get close and over the ball but stay slightly away to get under it.

While playing a grounded shot, the impact with the ball occurs during the downswing, with the face of the bat tilted slightly towards the ground. When you play a lofted shot, you hit the ball with the bat facing upwards. In theory, the lofted shot is an extension of the one played on the ground, but there is more to it; only a few players, like Matthew Hayden, can hit the quicker bowlers down the ground by simply extending and elevating the straight drive.

That is one difference between Hayden and Yusuf Pathan. While Hayden hits them with a straight bat, Pathan hits with a horizontal bat. The straight bat is a safer option because there is more room for error if you misread the bounce. By choosing horizontal strokes Pathan risks missing or edging the ball if it bounces more or less than he anticipated.

We have come a long way from the time when hitting sixes was a synonym for slogging. Hitting sixes on a regular basis is an art only a few have mastered. And those few are worth their weight in gold, especially in the T20 format.

THE ART OF CONTROLLING AN IPL GAME

The IPL is a bit like a Bollywood potboiler when Chennai Super Kings are playing. When the opponent and the scoreboard conspire against them, their star, M.S. Dhoni, marches in with an air of invincibility and bravado and raises his team from the dead. He is called the best finisher in T20 for a reason: when he is in the middle, one hardly ever doubts the result will not go CSK's way. That is how much sway he holds in the format.

His influence is not just restricted to when he contributes with the bat, but also when he dons the captain's hat. His meticulous manoeuvres on field suggest a dogged approach and an astute mind at work.

A T20 match unfolds at such a rapid pace that you need to look hard to notice the nuances. An IPL game unfolds even faster, or so it seems. The broadcasters cut to the cheerleaders after every four, six, or wicket, and focus on the players' wives and girlfriends and their reactions in between deliveries. So we rarely get to observe the little things that make an impact on the game. Captaincy is one such aspect that gets very little attention—unfortunately there isn't enough time to focus on the different field positions employed for various bowlers at different stages.

However, Dhoni's ingenious use of resources does catch the eye. Ironically a man who is usually reluctant to flirt with innovative field positions in ODIs and Tests is at his imaginative best in the IPL, especially when dealing with his India team-mates; he obviously knows a lot about their strengths and weaknesses and leaves no stone unturned when it comes to exploiting them.

Knowing Virat Kohli doesn't play the sweep shot remarkably well, especially early in his innings, made Dhoni place both short fine-leg and square leg inside the circle for R. Ashwin, an off-spinner. The fielding restrictions were off and there was no need to have those two men in the ring and risk a boundary, but Dhoni sensed a wicket taking opportunity and went with it. (Kohli didn't fall for it, though, which shows his maturity.)

Similarly, in the game against Delhi Daredevils in 2013, there was a concerted effort to bowl short and into Virender Sehwag's body, with a fielder manning the square-leg boundary. Dhoni knew that although Sehwag doesn't play the pull or hook shot that often, he could take the bait if pestered enough. And he did.

For Gautam Gambhir, Dhoni had a fifth slip throughout when the seamers were operating, primarily as a single-saving tactic, for Gambhir likes to play the dab shot through slips. He also had a fielder close, between point and cover, to restrict Gambhir's effective square drive. These may not be big tricks to bank on, but they make a huge difference in defining one's approach, and possibly the eventual outcome.

Dhoni plays with his field positions and bowling changes

more in T20s than in other formats, which betrays his affinity and comfort with the shorter version of the game. Also, his biggest strength, the ability to stay calm under pressure, is prominently visible in T20 cricket, for the other two formats run at a much slower pace. In fact, staying calm can be counterproductive at times in Test cricket, for you often need to set the pace of the game and not swim with the current.

> Bowling a yorker outside the off stump used to be an effective way to restrict Dhoni, for his bat-swing didn't allow him to go over cover that often, but even that isn't a safe option anymore.

The most common mistake a batsman makes while playing a T20 match is to submit to the pace of the game. The game may move at a heightened speed but one ought to remember that a bowler usually takes the same amount of time to run up and deliver as he does in any other format. Also, while big hitting may be the need of the hour, one needs to be aware that you can only hit the ball out of the park if you make the right contact, which means watching the ball till the last moment and not losing one's shape when hitting.

Dhoni ticks all these boxes, and more, while batting in the second half of a T20 innings. For starters, he has abandoned the pre-set batting order and usually walked in with about ten overs to spare (in T20 cricket, you don't go by the number of wickets that have fallen but the number of balls left). This has allowed him to bide his time a little. Then his acute game-sense leads him to rotate the strike for the early part, manoeuvre it to his advantage in the next few overs and own it in the final stretch of the game, displaying an immense self-belief in his skills to clear the fence at will.

From a technical vantage point, Dhoni's ability to not lose shape while playing the big shots sets him apart. He achieves this with legs that create a strong base, fast hands that generate phenomenal bat speed, a very unorthodox bat-swing that finishes with a twirl of the wrists (and not a full extension of his arms), and a tendency to hit with a relatively straight bat—he rarely goes too far across the stumps and doesn't target the square-leg boundary off the front foot.

In addition, he goes deep inside the crease to get under yorkers and create elevation. Bowling a yorker outside the off stump used to be an effective way to restrict Dhoni, for his bat-swing didn't allow him to go over cover that often, but even that isn't a safe option anymore: he has started waiting a little longer and playing them over the point region.

While batting, Dhoni's ability to not be flustered even when the asking rate is over twelve runs per over is fascinating; when his side is bowling, his tactical acumen to have fielders in positions that challenge batsmen to come out of their comfort zones shows his desire to be in complete control of the game. He knows when to go after bowlers, just as he knows when to shift gears, qualities that make him a rare asset in the T20 format.

SECTION FOUR

THE TALENTS

HOW WE ASSESS TALENT

In a country of over a billion people, talent ought to be as common as table salt. Why fuss over it? Especially talent in cricket, a game that is synonymous with sport in India and hence is intensely followed and widely played.

Clearly, though, that isn't the case, for had talent been so common, India would have been churning out prodigies all the time, sitting secure as the No. 1 Test-playing nation and ruling the other ICC rankings for years to come. Perhaps that is why talented cricketers are so revered—and rightly so. Rohit Sharma finds himself in this hallowed club, protected and persisted with to fortify his 'god-gifted talent', as M.S. Dhoni puts it.

In a sense, Rohit's talent has even superseded the intangible yet highly consequential yardstick of form, the lack of which is often responsible for a player being dropped from a team.

But isn't talent as intangible and indefinable as form? Talent means a special natural ability or aptitude, but who is to judge if that ability is special or ordinary? Wouldn't the answer be highly subjective? Our judgement of talent is often based on preconceived notions of what constitutes it, and thus, of who is 'talented'.

For instance, Sachin Tendulkar has been widely recognized as talented, but in comparison, not many would say the same for Anil Kumble—at least they wouldn't say that he was talented in the same measure as Tendulkar. Does that make him less talented?

From the beginning Tendulkar displayed special skills to successfully deal with all kinds of challenges thrown at him. He could do things others couldn't. He always seemed to have enough time to play the fastest bowlers on the fastest pitches. He had more than one stroke for every delivery. His timing and balance were superior to those of his peers and, above all, he had the ability to keep the good balls out and punish the bad balls consistently.

He had more time because he could pick the ball a fraction of a second earlier, which allowed him to get into the right position before the ball arrived. He had more strokes because he had supreme control over his bat's movements, and the extra time he had made that possible. His timing was also a gift, for he always knew precisely when to bring the bat down at the desired speed and angles. His ability to keep the good balls out, though, was not natural but nurtured.

On the other hand, Anil Kumble, who made his debut a year after Tendulkar, was first considered the antithesis of what a talented player should be. Unlike Tendulkar, who was marked as a 'special talent', Kumble fought a constant battle to prove people wrong, for leg-spinners of his type were not supposed to succeed beyond a point. The preconceived notions about talented leg-spinners were to do with their natural ability to get loop, drift in the air and vicious turn off the surface. Kumble ticked none of these boxes, for his height and high-arm action didn't allow him to create loop, nor did he spin the ball off the surface. He relied on unbelievable accuracy and subtle variations to create deception.

The jury could be divided on whether Kumble qualified as talented or whether his success was the result of sheer hard work. Even Rahul Dravid was rarely considered talented in his early days, for our notions about talented batsmen often have to do with flair and panache. The dogged approach to blunting an attack for sessions on end isn't what talent is all about—or so we are made to believe.

> In Kumble's or Dravid's case, not only did we fail to assess their talent fairly but we were also as quick to discredit it. What they possessed didn't match our understanding of talent.

But this is not about whether Rohit is talented or not. That, again, is a personal perception. The point I am making is simple: whether someone is permitted to or prohibited from making the cut shouldn't solely depend on our understanding of his talent, for our judgement of it could be skewed.

Tendulkar, the most gifted of cricketers, also became one of the most successful through hard work, not talent alone. An abundance of talent cannot automatically discipline the mind to be selective, something which is a crucial necessity.

While greatness can have a touch of predictability—and boredom—to it because it can't be achieved without a little bit of self-denial, talent is seldom boring. Talent allows you to do things others can't fathom.

That is not all. Tendulkar, with all his talent, needed to keep evolving as a batsman to remain one step ahead of the opposition. He wasn't the most technically correct player when he started out. He used to lean on his bat in his stance, which resulted in his head falling over and made him play across the line. He knew that to complement his talent and make the most of it, he needed to keep working on those little chinks in his game.

Over a period of time, the most talented batsman also became the most technically correct batsman. Talent put Tendulkar on the right path and his discipline took him to his destination.

The popular judgement of talent, in Tendulkar's case, was accurate, and fortunately he proved us right too. But as for Kumble or Dravid, not only did we fail to assess their talent fairly, we were also quick to discredit it. What they possessed didn't match our understanding of talent. They didn't have the flair (though they had the ability to concentrate for long hours). They didn't have two shots for the same ball, or a delivery that turned a lot, but they had the ability to be consistent in their approach. That, in my opinion, is also talent.

I grew up with many cricketers who were considered far more talented than I was, but most of them didn't even get to first-class level, let alone don the India cap. You might be justified in giving more opportunities to players at the junior level who are perceived to be talented, but we must acknowledge that talent doesn't always translate into success and that our understanding of talent can be slightly warped at times.

One may be tempted to give talented players a longer rope, but there is no guarantee that they will turn out to be successes. Vinod Kambli, at one time, was considered more talented than Tendulkar.

It is imperative to ensure, especially in a team sport, that players who are considered less talented are not given a rough deal in order to promote a talented player. It is tempting to find another Tendulkar, but that should not mean that the Dravids and Kumbles are not given a fair chance.

THE CONFIDENCE OF DHONI

In the dying overs of an ODI game, Iftiqar Anjum—the right-arm medium-pacer from Pakistan, moved the fine-leg fielder inside the circle. Next, and according to plan, he bowled a lethal yorker. Unabashedly, the batsman went down on one knee to sweep him past short fine leg. That was a tad too much for Anjum to abide by. Next ball, he sent the fine leg back to patrol the fence and brought in the third-man fielder inside the circle. This time, the batsman played a cheeky reverse-sweep past the short third-man fielder. While most batsmen would go on the defensive when the bowler is on the offensive, few, very few, retort in an equally or more aggressive and assertive fashion. This batsman did, then, and continuous to even now.

Mahendra Singh Dhoni may have, over the years been recognized for his gritty and unruffled sort of cricket, but it was this match—an India A encounter against Pakistan A in Kenya way back in 2004—with his two fours in two balls, that scripted the story of his years to come. As his teammate and as a spectator, it told me almost everything there was to know about this man. For starters, it was quite evident that Dhoni wasn't the one to fuss about copious technical jargons painstakingly etched in the many revered coaching manuals. That he would create his own rules—with an air of self-assurance, was for everyone to see.

The fact that his game wasn't built to please the purists parked in the plush President Box but for fans in the gallery, was unmistakable too. More importantly, it was Dhoni's raw passion and gusto that seemed to be defining each of his innings. Looking at him, one felt that he played for the sheer joy of it all.

It's ironic that Dhoni, ever since he's become the captain of the Indian cricket team, talks only about the process and not the results. That's a journey only a few take and accomplish.

From a technical vantage point, Dhoni's batting followed the simple principles of finding a way to score runs on every ball that was bowled to him. He built his initial game on his ability to clear the fence, for he had the strength to do it with aplomb against the slower bowlers. He refrained from using his feet too much to generate power to clear the fence and hence was always a difficult batsman to bowl to. It's a lot easier to bowl to a batsman who's a slave of his feet movement to generate power and momentum because often the eagerness to get close to the ball ends up in moving out a little earlier than one should, and that gives the bowler a chance to adjust. But if the batsman stays glued to his crease even when the intention is to take the aerial route, invariably the bowler falls into the trap. While he wasn't equally comfortable against the quicker bowlers in the beginning, he got better as his career progressed. There was something else, equally critical, which evolved at a rapid pace—his ability to read the game and change his game accordingly.

If you know that you can clear the fence at will, you often end up focusing and banking on that strength a bit too much.

So much so, that you completely ignore the importance of rotating the strike and playing the street-smart brand of cricket. Well, why wouldn't you, for taking six singles of six balls is a painstakingly slow and tiring process, especially when you can get as many off one ball. A batsman called Atul Bedade comes to my mind here—he had the gift of hitting sixes at will. Ironically, his international career got over before you could spell 'cricket' because he didn't have a second gear. But Dhoni's maturity belied his age, for he realized the importance of taking singles very early in his career. Even though he knew how to clear the fence, he would run between the wickets like his life depended on it. Even today, after all the wear and tear, he's still extremely fast between the stumps. He's also an astute judge of how many runs are on offer considering the strengths and weaknesses of the fielder pouncing on the ball—and that's a quality worth its weight in gold. In fact, during most team meetings, players settle on throwing to the other end when Dhoni is batting, simply because it's so difficult to keep up with his pace. No wonder we seldom see him falling short of the crease. He's also blessed with legs like tree-trunks, and that has little to do with the amount of time he spends in the gym. He isn't big on lifting a lot of weights or long distance running but focuses on sprints all the time. During the same India A tour of Zimbabwe and Kenya in 2004, he would invariably find ways to chicken out of running long-distance. He'd not only be the first to participate in the short sprints session, but would come first in every sprint that we ran. He admitted that he found running long-distance quite monotonous.

Fortunately, there's never a monotonous moment when he's in the middle with the willow in his hands, for the man is always on the move. While his legs are his best ally when it comes to running between the wickets, it's his hands that do most of the talking while batting, especially against the quicker bowlers. Playing spin is his strength and that's when his feet complement the hands to either get to the pitch of the ball or take him deep inside the crease to get more time to hit the short ball. He has both the brutal force to create a big shot out of nothing and also the finesse to place the ball between the two fielders at the deep for a quick couple of runs. Spare a moment of thought for the fielders stationed on the fence when Dhoni is batting, for half the time they're looking upwards and backwards to see the ball sail over their heads into the crowd, which pushes them right at the edge of the fence. And when they're sitting on the fence without taking a long start they're made to look like fools, for Dhoni steals a double by taking the pace off the ball. His astute sense of acceleration is the most fascinating part of his limited overs game, for he invariably starts slowly focusing only on ones and twos, then an occasional boundary to keep the required run rate—if batting second—in check and then he owns the strike to bludgeon everything that's sent his way. His batting is a perfect concoction of a butcher's strength and a surgeon's precision.

It's not just the slow bowling that he owns in the limited overs format, for even the world's quickest bowlers don't feel completely at ease while bowling to him in the death overs. Sample this—what would Dale Steyn or Lasith Malinga bowl to a set batsman in the death overs? It's quite straightforward that they'll use their extra pace to bowl bouncers and yorkers, and use the same pace as a decoy to slip in a few slower ones. Now, what are Dhoni's strengths? He's not the one who gets perturbed by bouncers; in fact, he's capable of hitting them for fours every time a bowler attempts that. He's found a unique way of clearing the front leg to get under the ball whenever a yorker is attempted, and his ability to stay very still at the crease in the death overs coupled with his arm-strength allows him to delay his shot without losing momentum or power the moment he spots a slower one. Since Dhoni has efficient responses to whatever a fast bowler can throw at him in the death overs, it's fair to say that his staying till the end is usually fruitful for the team he's batting for.

Batting in Test matches is a different kettle of fish though, for that's where his technique—or the lack of it—comes to the forefront and makes him fallible. Dhoni can play almost every shot that's there in the book; in fact, along the way he has also invented a few, like the helicopter shot. Yet, somehow he hasn't mastered the cover drive, and in my opinion, that's one shot a batsman can't do without. Most fast bowlers keep a few fielders in the slip cordon and bowl outside off (Test cricket allows them to drift further away from the batsman too) at a length that draws the batsman forward. There are only two shots that you can play on these deliveries—leave them alone for nothing, or drive through the covers for runs. Dhoni's basic instinct to attack and accumulate runs forces him to play the drive but his lack of feet movement keeps him a little away from the ball on most occasions, resulting in outside edges. He's predominantly a bottom-handed player and most of his strokes, even on the front foot through the off side bear an imprint of the bottom hand in action. Bottom hand domination coupled with lack of feet movement is the perfect recipe for disaster when playing an aggressive stroke off a fast bowler on a slightly helpful pitch. Also, the same can land you into trouble if the ball bends back in sharply after pitching because the front foot hasn't gone anywhere.

But you can always count on Dhoni to find a new way to deal with his limitations. He's coined quite a bizarre way of handling his weakness—he would walk across and down the pitch to get close the ball, even in a Test match. Moving so much takes him outside off and then even if he gets beaten by pace of a sharp in-dipper, he gets stuck outside off ruling out the leg-before dismissal. His method isn't foolproof and that's why he hasn't scored a single Test hundred outside the subcontinent but it's still good enough to make him stay relevant. In 2014, during India's last tour of England, he displayed another facet of his mental strength—he walked down the pitch and defended, took a lot of body blows and most importantly left a lot of balls alone. He spent close to twenty hours on the pitch in the five Test matches and showed that mental resolve can even take care of a slightly inferior technique.

Dhoni didn't feature much in the Zimbabwe leg of that India A tour. I would often find him bowling in the nets. As roommates we would get talking and I would tell him to be slightly greedy and bat in the nets, for his chance looked around the corner. His response was an offer—'I'll bowl to you also in the nets if you wish, and as far as my turn in the middle is concerned, I'll be fine.' The manner in which he uttered those words betrayed his mindset, for he wasn't arrogant about his chances but simply confident that he would succeed, and boy, wasn't he right! The foundation of his cricket is not just his unique technique, his astute cricket brain or his undeniably good luck. It is his belief in his own abilities that has brought him thus far.

HOW AGGRESSION PAYS OFF FOR McCULLUM

There are batsmen with exceptional bat speed, perfect timing and all the rest. And then there's Brendon McCullum. He possesses arguably the fastest hands in world cricket. If there are ways to gauge the speed of the ball after it leaves the bat, it wouldn't surprise me if the ball when hit by McCullum leaves faster than it arrived—and I'm talking about the fastest bowlers in the world.

It's one thing to bring your bat down in time and use the pace of the ball when the bowler is bowling fast. It's quite another to generate pace of your own while playing a fast bowler.

McCullum has quick feet to match his quick hands. Against spin you want to wait for the ball to leave the bowler's hand before dancing down the track—also, you can afford to—so that the spinner doesn't alter his line or length too much. But there's no such luxury against pace: once the fast bowler sees you step out, he has a few options. He can either shorten the length—to the extent of bowling a bouncer, or he can bowl fuller into the body, or do something else.

The trick to stepping out against spin is to get as close to the pitch of the ball as possible. It's important to meet the ball on the move to create momentum for big hits. But getting to the pitch of the ball is not possible against pace, and so the endeavour should be to form a stable base before the ball arrives. It's nearly impossible to play an aggressive shot against pace while the body is still on the move. In fact, most batsmen who use their feet against pace are prepared for the bowler to shorten the length, and so are ready to bring the flat-bat shots into play. When you bowl fuller to these batsmen, they end up defending awkwardly because they don't account for a full ball while stepping out. But McCullum steps out so often that bowlers don't always drag the ball short; they try other options. That's where his exceptional skills come to the fore. He has the rare ability to get under balls that are pitched full. And while batsmen usually have both hands close together on the bat, McCullum keeps his hands slightly apart, which allows him to use the bottom hand to scoop full deliveries over cover.

So that begs the question: is there a way to keep him quiet? Well, cricketing wisdom would suggest that you could bowl him full length, looking for swing—both in and outswing—for McCullum is extremely strong square of the wicket with his flat-batted shots. Also, since he's an opener, it's almost impossible to set a field for short-pitched deliveries, because if you target his ribcage with fine leg and square leg back, sooner rather than later you will err in line or he will make room to hit over the crowded off side circle. Even if he's hitting you off the front foot, it's wise to continue bowling full, with the option to bowl a bouncer once in a while.

In addition to his attacking mindset as a batsman, McCullum has been exceptional in the field as a captain. I believe he was easily the most attacking captain 2015 World Cup. The overriding theme of his captaincy is the intent to take wickets. He will put in as many as three slips against a new batsman if the ball is new and swinging. He will have fielders inside the circle to save singles and not to fulfil the requirements of having a certain number of fielders inside the circle either. He will make bowling changes in order to take wickets and not kill the middle overs.

He didn't let the game drift in any of New Zealand's matches in the World Cup. And the best part is that he isn't stubborn as a captain, for he's happy to rethink his plans if they aren't working. Against David Warner he started with fine leg inside the circle and the square leg fielder on the fence, but when he realized the ploy wasn't working, he changed it completely by getting his bowlers to bowl fuller slightly outside off stump.

His attacking approach is contagious. In the field he gives everything he has to save a run, an attitude that has rubbed on well to his teammates. New Zealand are the only team where everyone—including fast bowlers in the middle of a spell—dives to convert a half-chance into a wicket. The thought of 'what if I drop it' doesn't seem to cross the mind of this New Zealand team.

There doesn't seem to be a negative bone in McCullum's body, and his approach has made New Zealand punch above their weight. Who can forget their thrilling semi-final encounter against South Africa? McCullum's leadership and his teammates' killer instinct is precisely what took the Kiwis to the World Cup finals.

WHAT MAKES A.B. DE VILLIERS TICK

A.B. de Villiers jumped across, and Andre Russell followed him with an intended yorker that ended up as a low full toss. De Villiers went down on one knee and played a scoop-sweep over the head of the fielder at short fine-leg for a six.

In another over, he threatened to move across with his back foot but withdrew at the last minute; Jason Holder decided to target the stumps this time, to which de Villiers reverse-swept him for a one-bounce four over the gully region.

Some of the shots de Villiers manages to pull off these days fall in the 'unbelievable' category. The bat he uses weighs well over a kilogram, but he moves it like a wand. How does he do it, seeming to defy the fundamentals of batting, writing his own rules for future generations to follow?

Big hitting has a few basics. The head must stay still at all times, especially before and while the shot is being played. The body must remain stable and maintain shape after executing the shot. And the body must allow the bat to swing freely, by moving away or adopting an angle to avoid interrupting the flow of the bat.

The notable thing about de Villiers' batting is the stillness of his head. While most people talk about his incredible bat speed, he focuses a lot on keeping his head still even when he's on the move—and he's on the move quite a lot. Regardless of whether he is jumping across the stumps to prepare for a scoop or stepping down the pitch to take on the bowler, his head is poised. His body moves but not his head. The stillness of the head allows him to follow the path of the ball till the last possible moment, and that facilitates the playing of defensive and attacking shots.

The second striking feature is his stability at the crease. You need a strong base to execute big shots; they say that to generate maximum power both your feet should be firmly grounded, for that allows you to use gravity to your advantage. Like most South Africans, de Villiers too has a back-and-across trigger movement, but unlike others he crouches a little while preparing for the ball to arrive. By doing so, he lowers his centre of gravity, and that leads to greater stability. A stable base is necessary to create power. Whenever he wants to hit these extraordinary shots, de Villiers stays low, broadens the base by keeping his legs apart, and maintains his shape while hitting.

A perfect yorker is almost impossible for any batsman to get away. That's why the differentiator is a player's ability to hit slightly off-target yorkers—the ones that fall a few inches shorter than intended. De Villiers' low hands allow him to get under the deliveries that other batsmen struggle to dig out.

He also has the extraordinary ability to go down on one knee and play the scoop shot. While the helmet has made it possible for modern batsmen to contemplate these adventurous shots, there aren't many who can attempt them against genuine quick bowlers. The ones who do try to pull them off usually have their eyes closed at the point of impact because their head is moving, but that's not the case with de Villiers. His ability to change his shot at the last minute shows that he is able to keep his eye on the ball for longer than other batsmen. Also, he makes sure he is positioned optimally while attempting the shot: he clears the front leg and tilts his body a little to open up the area behind square on the leg side when he wants to hit finer, for getting inside the line isn't always possible against a fast bowler's attempted yorker.

So is it possible to bowl to him and get away relatively unscathed?

While there isn't a foolproof method of getting the better of A.B. when he's in full flow, there are some things a bowler can attempt to minimize damage.

Whenever de Villiers jumps across and goes down on one knee, bowlers tend to follow him; that is the basic instinct of a bowler confronted with a moving batsman: follow him. That's just what de Villiers wants the bowler to do, so it's imperative to resist the temptation and bowl at the stationary target: the stumps. It may still go for a four or a six but in case he misses, you give yourself a chance.

Also, I find it surprising that not many bowlers bowl a bouncer when he jumps across, for de Villiers isn't really prepared for that ball at that moment. When you are crouched low down on the back knee, you're not in the ideal position to play the hook or pull. I can understand that it's easier said than done with the new rules of having five fielders inside the circle but it's still worth trying. We've all seen the outcome when bowlers go through the motions instead.

VERY VERY SPECIAL LAXMAN

As I look back to my first memories of V.V.S. Laxman, a scene from a South Zone vs North Zone Duleep Trophy game in January 2001 plays itself out vividly in my mind.

There were about fifteen international cricketers playing in that game, and clearly the quality of cricket was top-notch. Though heaps of runs were scored, it was Laxman's love for refined cricket, which he played with the utmost subtlety and culture, and his supreme skill, that remains etched in my mind till this day. Such was his aura that a teammate had to point out that instead of cheering for our bowlers and egging our team on, I was celebrating Laxman's fine display. It is hard to not be influenced and inspired by greatness.

Laxman had been striking two or three boundaries every over without breaking a sweat, and it felt as if getting smacked all over the park was a small price to pay to witness something truly spectacular. That is what Laxman did all his life to his teammates and opposition—while his teammates appreciated his craft, the opposition wished they could be on his side.

Standing in that lonely slip position that day, I was made aware of the fact that a seemingly orthodox, unadventurous-seeming, rather reticent-looking man could play revolutionary cricket; that the belief that cricket is an extension of one's personality wasn't always true. Laxman had made his nonconformist style look like a chapter from the coaching manual—one that the guidebook had been forced to include.

Working the angles

Most young batsmen are taught that the easiest way to bat is to play the ball back in the direction it came from, which basically means playing it with a straight bat. Once you grow as a batsman, you learn to play with the swing and spin, which is an extension of playing with the straight bat. You further learn to either play a little early or to delay the stroke to find gaps, but you are always advised not to play across the line or against the spin or swing.

Laxman turned these fundamentals on their head by not only showing that meeting the ball with an angled bat produces desirable results but also proving that playing with the spin and swing is overrated. Though his style of play made batting look ever so easy, if inspected in detail, it was nothing less than an engineering marvel, for he worked out the angles astutely.

During cricket training, you are always advised not to play against the spin, especially when a bowler of Shane Warne's quality is bowling into the rough, but Laxman showed that you can—with good results too—if you close the face of the bat at precisely the time of impact (and not a fraction earlier, like more ordinary batsmen tend to do, resulting in return catches). By doing so, he created extraordinary angles, piercing the well-guarded on-side field. His ability to create these angles by, at times, bringing the bat down at a slight incline, or using his supple wrists, enabled him to find gaps where others found fielders. Muttiah Muralitharan, another champion bowler, said that Laxman could potentially play shots on either side of the wicket to any given ball, which made it impossible for a captain to set fields for him.

Playing it late

Most batsmen who are extremely strong off the legs have a technical deficiency that forces their head to fall slightly towards the off side in the stance. The moment the head falls, the judgement of lines gets blurred. This results in hitting balls pitched on off-middle towards the on side. Essentially, these players' affinity for the on side is a by-product of a technical flaw.

Laxman's preference for the on side, though, was by design, and he was equally fluent through the off side. His supple wrists and his ability to delay a shot till the last possible instant allowed him to hit balls pitched on middle stump to the right of the square-leg umpire. This is perhaps the most difficult shot to create, because if you don't find the pinpoint precision necessary, you're doomed. You not only have to delay the shot when attempting this stroke, you also need to close the bat face completely (almost showing the edge of the bat to the bowler), and yet hit the ball from the middle.

This became a routine; just when the bowler thought the ball was going to elude Laxman, because he looked visibly late on it, the bat would come down. If Laxman had delayed his shots by even a fraction more than he did, the ball would have hit his body or the stumps. Such was his pristine timing.

Economy of movement

As expansive as Laxman's hand movements were, he was frugal when it came to moving his feet to reach the pitch of the ball, for he could make up for it with his hands. The lack of movement made him extremely still at the crease, which meant that he was rarely off balance. The lack of foot movement created room for his arms and hands to work freely, which made him a free-flowing batsman when in form. The flip side of reaching the ball with hands—and not feet—was that it didn't look very compact when he was out of form, like he played in Australia on his last tour.

Laxman's cricket has been a paradox of a zen-like façade and a fighter's instinct within. Perhaps that is what makes him one of the most intriguing cricketers of our times. His batting has been a viewer's delight and many Laxman innings have been spectacular cricket extravaganzas. Some of his shots deserve a statutory warning: these stunts have been performed by an expert, please don't try them at home!

MITCHELL JOHNSON

The bowler runs in hard, sends down a bouncer and makes the batsman hop and duck. With his feet in the air from the hop and his head tucked into his chest from the attempt at ducking, he manages to stay away from the line of the ball. The wicketkeeper, standing close to the thirty-yard circle, makes a futile attempt to get an outstretched hand to the ball, which thuds into the sightscreen after bouncing once inside the rope.

The bowler: Mitchell Johnson. The batsman: Sanju Samson. The event: a Champions League match in Jaipur in 2013.

The sight of a fast bowler making a batsman hop gets you to sit up and watch intently. And if the bowler makes some of the best batsmen in the world duck and sway on docile Indian pitches, you hold your breath in anticipation whenever that bowler runs in to bowl.

It is evident that Johnson has picked up his pace in the last couple of years. And while the increase in pace is visibly upsetting batsmen, one must note that the late inward movement into right-handers, and the bounce, are also playing havoc.

In the ODI series against India in early 2015, Johnson had troubled the Indian batsmen with the same extra bounce and pace, on pitches where totals of 300-plus have been par for the course. It is not that the Indians had not faced this kind of pace or bounce; on the contrary, they have played it with authority and even dominated it in the past. But Johnson was a slightly different proposition. If you don't believe me, ask the England cricket team.

He isn't the typical left-arm fast bowler who bowls with a high-arm action and relies mostly on exploiting the natural angle lefties create while bowling to right-handers. His bowling arm is some distance away from his left ear, and that makes it difficult for batsmen to gauge the bounce he will generate after pitching.

For bowlers with high-arm actions, the bounce off the surface is directly related to their point of release, which makes for a certain predictability. But with bowlers who have a slinging action, it is relatively difficult to assess how much bounce they will get after pitching. Such bowlers skid the ball off the surface, unlike the ones with high-arm actions. When you bowl with a high-arm action, the bounce you get is similar to that of tennis ball when it drops on a dry surface, and with a sling-arm action it is a bit like the bounce of a plastic ball on a wet surface.

Have you ever tried making a stone skip on water? The lower the arm while throwing, the higher the frequency of the stone bouncing off the surface of the water. Another key difference with regard to bounce is the trajectory of the ball after pitching—for bowlers with a high-arm action, the ball gains considerable height right after pitching, but for someone with a round-arm action, the path is more gradual, similar to an aeroplane taking off: it is not easy to gauge when the ball has reached the peak of its bounce. (This is why even wicketkeepers don't know how far back they should stand.)

Then there is the small matter of whether the ball lands on the seam or on the shine. If it lands on the seam, it bounces considerably more than it would if it lands on the leather. When a bowler delivers with a round-arm action, even he can't be 100 per cent sure of making the ball land on the seam, so what chance does the poor batsman have?

> A round-arm action puts severe pressure on the lower back and hips, which could lead to serious injuries. Mitchell Johnson's impact comes with a disclaimer: try to imitate it at your own peril.

Johnson's natural bowling action is designed to make the ball curve in to the right-hand batsman, and when he's on top of his game, the ball comes in sharply. While the ball that moves laterally creates its own challenges—the batsman must not commit, must play close to the body—in Johnson's case, the ones that don't move create similar problems as well.

Given his round-arm action, which makes the ball curve in mostly, batsmen tend to play inside the line most times, so the ones that hold their line and go across cause trouble. When the ball doesn't come out right from Johnson's hand, it doesn't swing and carries on across and away from the right-hander. Also, even when it comes out right, if Johnson has started a little too far outside off, the ball doesn't swing and carries on across the right-hander. There is a thin line outside a right-hander's off stump that the bowler must adhere to, so that the ball can curve in effectively. Johnson inadvertently crosses that line from time to time, keeping the batsman guessing.

Won't rookies be tempted to start out bowling with a round-arm, slingy action, given the obvious benefits of doing so? My advice in this regard is that it is important to know the flip side of such an action before taking the plunge. We only hear about the ones who have fought the odds and reached the top. It is important to know the rules to break them. Many bowlers with similar actions have ended up with severe back problems. A round-arm action puts severe pressure on the lower back and hips, which could lead to serious injuries. Also, it is not easy to be accurate regularly with such an action. Mitchell Johnson's impact comes with a disclaimer: try to imitate it at your own peril.

THE KOHLI METHOD

When they first donned the Indian colours, the likes of M.S. Dhoni and Yuvraj Singh were self-assured, resilient, fiercely talented and more. Today, Virat Kohli seems to have outdone his predecessors in a manner that has made him the face of Indian cricket's next generation. He has scored twenty-two centuries in 158 ODI matches. Those are phenomenal numbers by any yardstick. Look closer, in a comparative framework, and the numbers hit harder. Kumara Sangakkara, for instance, has scored twenty-five hundreds in 404 ODIs and Virender Sehwag had scored fifteen in 251 matches. These stats, striking as they are, tell us a thing or two about the sort of prospect Kohli is for Indian cricket.

If one goes by the exterior—the spiky hair, tattoos, the swagger and arrogance of a confident young man, Kohli epitomises twenty-first century Indian youth. But the way he bats, especially in the first half of each innings, he seems the antithesis of how young cricketers in India like to bat in this day and age of T20 cricket. These days most young men prefer to go after the bowling right from the beginning, and to keep hitting it till they last. It takes your breath away when it comes off, and looks woeful when it doesn't, but taking a bit of a risk seems to be the new way of living.

Kohli, on the contrary, is old-fashioned when it comes to constructing his innings. Regardless of his personal form, familiarity with the attack and the conditions, he always starts slowly, albeit confidently. At the beginning of an innings, every batsman is slightly edgy and likes to get bat on ball and score a few to get going. This urge to get on with the game is even stronger if you are in good form. It must take immense self-control for Kohli to resist that temptation every time he walks out to bat these days and to stick to his original plan of biding time.

This self-control at the beginning of every innings is the primary reason for his consistency. Exercising this self-control would be a lot easier for someone who doesn't have as many shots as Kohli does, which makes his self-denial more creditable. His ability to plan meticulously and then diligently follow the plan is the common thread in most of his innings.

Conventional wisdom suggests that the bigger the arc one's bat creates, the more power one generates. The arc starts from the top of the backlift and finishes with the follow-through after playing the shot. The best way to ensure a bigger arc is to allow the top hand to remain in control for as long as possible and extend the arms fully (elbow not bent) after playing the shot. Kohli's bat-swing, however, is not quite how the coaching manuals say it ought to be. He has a relatively short backlift, and an even shorter follow-through. But he generates phenomenal bat speed by flicking his wrists at the point of contact, which in turn generates immense power. The flip side of such a bat-swing is that he is a bottom-hand dominated player. Once again though, by delaying his strokes, he has found a way to be equally fluent through the off side.

When I saw Kohli for the first time, I was a little sceptical about his short front-foot stride. To make matters more complicated, that short stride was going far too across. While the short and across front-foot stride allowed him to whip balls pitched on the middle through the on side, it also made him slightly susceptible to full-pitched swinging deliveries, or when the ball deviated appreciably off the pitch.

During one of our conversations while playing for Delhi, I told him about my observations. He assured me that he had found a way around it, which was by allowing the ball to come to him. I saw merit in his method of dealing with the shortcoming, but I wasn't fully convinced that it would work at the highest level.

By scoring twenty-two ODI hundreds while batting at No. 3, Kohli has certainly proved that his solution works just fine. It also proves that technique is slightly overrated at times. In fact, his method of overcoming his technical deficiency is his biggest strength: playing very late. By allowing the ball to come to him, he is able to find the gaps more often. Playing the ball right under his eyes also ensures that he misses fewer deliveries, and so the perils of the short front-foot stride are taken care of.

He may still find it slightly difficult when the ball is pitched up in seaming conditions like it did in England in the summer of 2014. The thing that has separated him from the rest is his ability to constantly improve. He was a sitting duck against the short-pitched stuff when he had started, so much so, that even on docile Indian pitches, bowlers like Ashish Nehra and Munaf Patel got him out whenever they wanted with a well-directed bouncer. Even his Test career started on a sour note when West Indies bowlers bounced him out on his maiden Caribbean tour. He was duly dropped from the next Test tour to England in 2011. But that is a thing of the past, for now he is not only comfortable against the short ball but also is one of the most aggressive Indian batsmen against that length, even on bouncy and faster overseas pitches. Dravid told me that a good way to judge a player's evolution is to observe if he is repeating the same mistakes he used to commit earlier, and both of us agreed that Kohli was very good at not falling in the same ditch again. That makes me reasonably optimistic about his chances for his next tour to England. I won't be surprised if he comes back as the highest run scorer in all formats.

WHAT MAKES MAXWELL DIFFERENT

What are the chances of seeing, even in a T20 game, a reverse sweep being played by a batsman to a ball pitched a couple of feet outside leg? While the shot is often lucrative towards the end of an innings, how many batsmen would be audacious enough to try it if there were more overs left in the game than had been bowled?

Glenn Maxwell is one such player who is rewriting the rules of batting in the shorter formats of the game. The shot mentioned above was played against R. Ashwin in Kings XI Punjab's first IPL game last year. ESPNcricinfo's ball-by-ball commentary described it in this way:

3.2 *Ashwin to Maxwell, FOUR, no need to get your eye in, just pull out that reverse sweep and drag the carrom ball from way outside leg stump to the point boundary. That is just a top shot.*

Maxwell played a few more fours after that one, with equal success. Still, there are a few batsmen who, in spite of being phenomenally good in T20, find it tough to translate that success to the fifty-over game, for they simply do not have the game to take on quality bowlers who aren't hamstrung by being able to bowl only four overs a game. Most batsmen who are T20 successes are lethal against lesser bowlers, and reasonably aggressive against better bowlers, but if a quality bowler is allowed to have an extended spell against them, they are found out. However, though Maxwell is not a runaway success in ODIs yet, his knock against England in the tri-series final and against India in the warm-up game are a fair indicator of what to expect from him in the World Cup. While he might not be the standout performer for Australia—he plays in a side with proven match-winners in it, and bats too low to make a regular impact—he is likely to play a few crucial knocks when they matter.

What are the chances of seeing, even in a T20 game, a reverse sweep being played by a batsman to a ball pitched a couple of feet outside leg? While the shot is often lucrative towards the end of an innings, how many batsmen would be audacious enough to try it if there were more overs left in the game than had been bowled?

Like a lot of modern batsmen, Maxwell has quick hands that allow him to generate great bat speed. It's a quality that's needed if you aren't built like Chris Gayle or Kieron Pollard. There's no substitute for hitting the ball hard once it gets old and the field spreads. While there's still a lot of merit in putting the ball in gaps and running hard, 300-plus in an ODI and 200-plus in a T20 can't be achieved without hitting fours and sixes, and Maxwell is good at it.

What makes Maxwell different from most players is the fact that he doesn't play the bowler or the ball that is bowled to him but the field that has been set for him. Once he's reasonably confident about his form on the day, his choice of strokes is totally a reaction to where the fielders are. The reverse sweep I mentioned earlier was a result of the point fielder being inside the circle to Ashwin. So Maxwell had to either beat the inner ring or hit over it. Yes, there's still a lot of risk because of the lack of complete control while playing a reverse sweep, because of the angles involved, but Maxwell isn't one to fuss over percentages.

That's another quality most batsmen who pull off these unorthodox shots share—they are completely convinced that they will pull it off almost every single time. Virender Sehwag would play Muttiah Muralitharan against the spin all the time with a conviction that the ball wouldn't go through the gap between bat and pad. If it did, he'd consider it an aberration and play against the spin again when Murali came on. Sometimes you envy these players' mindsets; most 'thinking' cricketers spend their time wondering about what will happen if they don't connect.

If the third-man fielder is inside the circle, it is almost a given that Maxwell will attempt a reverse sweep sooner rather than later. If the point fielder is inside to a fast bowler, Maxwell will attempt an inside-out shot, backing away. The good thing about playing the gaps is that he doesn't need to hit a seventy-yard shot every time, and since he only needs to clear the thirty-yard circle, he doesn't hit the ball too hard, which means he can maintain shape on most occasions. Reading the field also gives you an insight into the bowler's plan. For example, if the third-man and fine-leg fielders are inside the circle, the bouncer is out of the question; instead a slower one is much more likely. If the mid-off fielder is inside the circle to a fast bowler, you don't expect full balls.

Obviously it's not easy to reverse-sweep a fast bowler, or to hit him down the ground if it is short, but the rewards are worth the risk. Maxwell has received a fair amount of criticism for throwing his wicket away when ten to twelve overs are still left in the game, but that's the nature of the beast. You can't play high-risk, low-percentage cricket and score big hundreds regularly. Also, given his batting position, he's not really required to score hundreds; his job is to maximize the scoring potential.

While there are many things that are going Maxwell's way at the moment, teams might want to look at the chinks in his game. For starters, he isn't 100 per cent comfortable against good quick bouncers, so opposition attacks may want to look at using the big grounds in Australia to lay traps. Maxwell gets away with playing attacking shots against bouncers in the IPL because of the slower pitches and smaller grounds, but he might get into trouble if he tries the same things in Australia. It won't be a bad idea to throw the ball to your fastest bowler when Maxwell walks in.

The second ball that's likely to work is the yorker. Targeting the nose and toes is fairly established as a successful tactic in the death overs, but with Maxwell you cannot afford to wait till the death overs, because he gets going as soon as he walks in to bat. If you allow him to find his feet, chances are you'll end up paying a huge price.

UNRAVELLING SUNIL NARINE'S MYSTERY

It is hard for anything to remain a mystery today, what with all the footage available via replays in slow-motion; every player, every ball, every stroke is painstakingly scrutinised. When it comes to match analysis, the action has shifted from the twenty-two-yard stretch to the editing table. Yet, Sunil Narine continues to beat technology and stay ahead of most analyses. Even though he has been scanned time and again, he manages to get the better of batsmen and fascinate spectators.

He is not the first mystery spinner; there have been quite a few batsmen who couldn't decipher him immediately, if at all. Yet there is something about this lad from the West Indies, with a peculiar hairdo and an equally peculiar action, that has enthralled aficionados worldwide.

In his debut IPL season, Narine took twenty-four wickets and helped Kolkata Knight Riders win the trophy for the first time. But it isn't just his ability to take wickets that makes everyone sit up and take note, it is the way he spins around hapless batsmen.

One particular over that he bowled to his fellow Caribbean

teammate Andre Russell in the opening match of IPL-6 comes to mind, because it looked like the batsman had no idea which way the ball would turn after pitching. Each time almost, he played down one way when the ball was heading the other.

It is not too hard to decipher a doosra or a carrom ball from an off-spinner while watching on TV, when the camera gives us the view from the back, but Narine's variations are hard to pick even for viewers sitting at home. So what chance did Russell have?

By bowling even his off-spinners with a scrambled seam, Narine manages to keep the batsman guessing which one will head the other way. And since he bowls both his variations from the front of the hand (the doosra is usually bowled from the back of the hand), you have to look very closely which way his fingers are turning at the point of release. That is not an easy job.

But it isn't just the variations or his ability to disguise them that make Narine a difficult bowler to bat against in T20. There are many bowlers who have more variations up their sleeve. All good leg-spinners have three deliveries (leg spin, googly and flipper) and most off-spinners these days also possess more than a couple variations (off spin, doosra and a carrom ball), but it isn't about the quantity, it is about the quality of execution. Having different types of deliveries won't mean much unless you know when to use them.

In fact, Narine has only two variations in his bag—a regular off-spinner and the one that goes away after pitching. But unlike other spinners, he is a master when it comes to using his subtle variations and he rarely overdoes them.

In his first over in IPL 6, he did not bowl a single away-going delivery. He realized that there was some turn and bounce on the Eden Gardens pitch, so he was better off bowling off breaks.

In fact, in the entire game, he didn't bowl a single away-going delivery to the well-set Mahela Jayawardene, having arranged a leg-side field for him. If Jayawardene had picked the variation, Narine would have run the risk of leaking runs. But against Russell, Narine strengthened the off-side field, with a slip as an attacking option, and bowled the other one repeatedly. His ability to judge the demands of the situation and then move from being smart and defensive to brave and aggressive sets him apart.

In addition to his gaming sense and variety, Narine's pace and his effective stock ball make it very tough to score off him. He bowls really flat and slightly quicker but without compromising on turn off the surface. If there is something in the pitch for the spinners, he really rips them across the right-handers and away from the left-handers.

The delivery that got David Warner in the slips in the same game was an example of his ability to turn the ball with bounce at reasonably high speed. His pace and flat trajectory take away the batsman's crucial attacking strategy—stepping down the track to play the lofted shot. There aren't many who can hit the long ball without coming out of the crease.

If you can't come down the track, you look to either slog-sweep towards midwicket or go deep into the crease to pull the slightly shorter deliveries. Narine's extra turn and bounce on pitches like the one at the Eden Gardens make both these shots tough to execute. The turn ensures the ball misses the bat's sweet spot. If that fails, the bounce ensures the ball's impact on the bat is higher than the batsman is comfortable with. Either way, the batsman rarely gets the intended height or distance.

If batsmen look for five or six runs off a Narine over instead of going after him, he might not turn out to be such a prolific wicket taker. Unfortunately for all IPL teams, Knight Riders captain Gautam Gambhir brings Narine on either in the powerplay or during the death overs. That forces batsmen to go after Narine and increases his chances of picking up wickets. I won't be surprised if he finishes as one of the top wicket takers in the history of the IPL.

WHY MALINGA IS NOT A THREAT ANY MORE

Since his Test debut in 2004, Lasith Malinga has been one of the most discussed bowlers in international cricket, his unusual action causing great curiosity, though it has never been formally questioned. Like most players, Malinga is a product of his environment. His youth was spent playing tennis-ball cricket on the beach, where he adapted his skills and bowling action to suit his environment, producing a unique kind of delivery that limited the bounce of a tennis ball and allowed him to hit the target more often.

The only time I faced Malinga was in a three-day warm-up match on India A's tour to Sri Lanka in 2002. On seeing his low-slung action, Gautam Gambhir and I realized we had to watch his hand closely and keenly, for there seemed to be very little conventional method to his bowling. He was generating disconcerting speed and bounce, and without any clues in his action about what line or length he would achieve, our job remained tough. But because it was early in his career, he was still quite erratic; both Gambhir and I tackled him well and managed to get centuries in that match. Little did we know that Malinga was on his way to establish himself as one of the most dangerous bowlers in the world.

The most important trick to batting is in picking the line and length early, because it helps you get into the right position. The only way to gauge the length is to focus on the point of release—the earlier the release, the fuller the ball. To judge the line, focus on the wrist and the bowler's position on the crease. If the wrist is tilted towards third man and the bowler is very close to the stumps, the educated guess is that the line will be around off stump, since the bowler is trying is to move the ball away from the batsman. If the wrist facing fine leg and the bowler is operating wide of the crease, the ball is likely to slant into the batsman. While the method to gauge length is foolproof, there are exceptions to the rule when judging line. Since there is hardly any time to react after the ball is delivered, most batsmen hedge their bets on following these principles, albeit with a hint of caution.

These rules are relatively easy to follow for orthodox bowlers, whose actions are more predictable, with their bowling arms close to the ear. As a batsman, it takes a lot of time to get used to watching Malinga's bowling hand from in front of the umpire's face.

His accuracy in bowling toe-crushing reverse swinging yorkers and his ability to bowl bouncers and well-disguised slower ones have been impressive. Unfortunately, like with most freak actions, after a few years in international cricket, Malinga was exposed. Once the novelty wore off, batsmen found ways to judge his line and length and the level of difficulty reduced considerably.

But deception wasn't Malinga's only weapon. A good yorker

or bouncer are still tough deliveries to counter. The flip side was that Malinga was at his best only when he bowled either of the two.

Today, because he doesn't hit the pitch with an upright seam consistently, his good-length balls are not difficult to handle. In seam-friendly conditions, where even lesser bowlers thrive, Malinga finds it tough to be as effective, because since the ball doesn't land on the seam, it doesn't dart around enough.

The introduction of a new ball from either end in an ODI innings since October 2011 has only compounded Malinga's problems. While he remains effective with the new ball, his performance dips considerably in the middle and death overs because neither ball gets old enough even towards the end of the innings.

Malinga in ODIs	Inns	Overs	Wkts	Best	Avg	Econ	S/R
Overall	178	1476.5	283	6/38	27.31	5.23	31.3
October 2011 onwards	88	721.1	134	5/32	29.85	5.54	32.2
Till September 2011	90	755.4	149	6/38	25.03	4.93	30.4

His reverse swinging toe-crushers are not finding their mark as consistently as they used to. Any quality bowler will confirm that it is far more difficult to find the blockhole with a newish ball as compared to an old one. Even when Malinga does find the target with the relatively new ball, the lack of reverse swing makes it easier for the batsman to get under it. His slower deliveries have also been affected by the rule. While earlier the off break variation of the slower ball would grip the surface and bounce a lot more off it, now the lack of grip off the pitch takes the sting away.

Phase-wise Period	First 15			15.1 to 40			40.1 to 50		
	Avg	Econ	S/R	Avg	Econ	S/R	Avg	Econ	S/R
Jan 2010–30 Sep 2011	27.38	4.47	43.38	23.00	4.90	30.59	9.38	4.63	11.58
October 2011 onwards	28.95	4.73	36.7	45.72	5.81	47.19	19.13	6.56	17.49

Players like Virat Kohli and M.S. Dhoni have started to decipher Malinga's once mysterious bowling with ease. Batsmen who stay low in their stance are better equipped to counter the lower trajectory of Malinga's deliveries. It also helps to shorten your backlift while dealing with reverse-swinging yorkers. Generally, when batsmen sacrifice their backlift, they sacrifice power, but Kohli and Dhoni have the ability to generate enough bat speed and thereby get power into their shots by flicking their wrists. They are also able to get the better of Malinga because they are good on the leg side, thanks to their strong wrists, and go deep inside the crease to get under his yorkers.

Malinga has pushed the boundaries of convention long enough to finally be admired and not admonished. Watching him in action has made me believe that cricket isn't entirely a batsman's game, after all. The introduction of two new balls in ODIs was expected to trouble the spinners, but it has adversely affected Malinga too. In eleven innings in the CB Series in Australia in February–March 2012, Malinga took eighteen wickets at a strike rate of thirty-five, with an economy rate of above six, and it wasn't surprising that he wasn't the same threat in the 2015 World Cup.

ACKNOWLEDGEMENTS

I would like to express my gratitude to the many people who saw me through this book—Sambit Bal, Sharda Ugra and many others at ESPNcricinfo India for providing support, talking things over, offering comments and assisting me in giving my readers an insightful copy each time.

V.K. Karthika, thank you for believing in this book. Without your creative supervision and encouragement, and your team's best efforts, this book couldn't have been written to its fullest.

Most of all though, I wish to thank my mentor, Mr Tarak Sinha—'Ustaad Ji' as we at the Sonnet Cricket Club fondly call him—for taking a seven-year-old under his wings and sharing with him his best lessons on cricket and life. I owe every bit of my cricket to you, sir, and this book is just an extension of all that I learnt from you in over two decades.

Mum and Dad, had it not been for you, I may not have been a cricketer. Thank you for keeping my dreams before yours, every single time.

Aekta, I know you're keeping an eye on your little brother

from the world up above. Thank you for being my guiding angel, always.

Aakshi, thank you for letting me write even when we're on vacation; for sitting through all those brainstorming sessions for the next column; for being the listener you are, and for proofreading my articles even when cricket is mostly Greek to you.